STRATEGISTS FIRST

HOW TO DEFEAT THE STRATEGY TRAP

RYAN HAYS

POST HILL PRESS

A POST HILL PRESS BOOK
ISBN: 979-8-88845-176-2
ISBN (eBook): 979-8-88845-177-9

Strategists First:
How to Defeat the Strategy Trap
© 2023 by Ryan Hays
All Rights Reserved

Cover design by Conroy Accord

Post Hill Press
New York • Nashville
posthillpress.com

Published in the United States of America
1 2 3 4 5 6 7 8 9 10

"When I was young, a teacher had forbidden
me to say 'more perfect' because she said
if a thing is perfect it can't be more so.

But by now I had seen enough of life to
have regained my confidence in it."

—NORMAN MACLEAN

This book is dedicated to Lori, Avalyn, and Wil.

You have always been more perfect to me.

TABLE OF CONTENTS

2 FIXES

1 MISSION

0 DOUBT

PREFACE

This book makes no references to I, we, or me. And there's a reason for that.

Too many leadership and strategy books double as revisionist history. When authors bring their past to the page, their stories tend to autocorrect their memories, recasting their experiences in more augmented ways. Their vision becomes more visionary, insights more insightful, successes more successful, and strategies more strategic.

Never is the aim to deceive. The intent is pure, and the facts are real. But the stories that carry them are tricky to manage, especially when the author casts themselves as the narrator. Stories are performances. And performances are more made than found. Given the innate desire to entertain, stories have a way of aggrandizing themselves.

The goal isn't to declare war on stories. This book employs plenty of them.

The concern is with self-narrated stories. The ones that tempt authors to spend more time curating their past than serving your present. By narrating such stories, authors become the story. It's too much about them. Not enough about you.

A book should be able to transport the reader to a better place without forcing them to carry the author's baggage.

Leadership and strategy books should focus on you. And relentlessly so.

What content best serves you? What questions challenge you? What stories inspire you? What habits must you learn and unlearn? Which key thinkers and theories should you know? How can this book be helpful beyond your initial read?

It's about what the reader needs to hear, not what the author wants to say. "Say books" belong to a different time and place. This is a "need book." It's designed to get you where you need to go—smarter, faster, and better. Here's how.

The writing is lean. *There is more value in fewer words.*

The chapters are concise. *Read them between meetings.*

The content is practical. *Use these learnings and un-learnings right now.*

The strategy is simple. *Make you a lifelong strategist.*

The novelist Franz Kafka believes "a book must be the axe for the frozen sea inside us."[1] If this book becomes your axe for the frozen sea of strategy, it has done its job.

INTRODUCTION

Ever wonder why you've had more strategy conversations than you can count, but not a single strategist discussion you can remember?

You're not alone. Most individuals and organizations focus on *strategy*, not *strategists*.

Welcome to the strategy trap.

The strategy trap is easy to explain but hard to escape. It operates by prioritizing strategy and deprioritizing the strategist. *Translation: strategy is the rock star that gets idolized; strategists are the roadies that get ignored.*

Skeptical? When was the last time you read a book on strategists, not strategy?[2] When was the last time your organization invested in strategists, not strategy? How many academic programs center on strategists, not strategy?

Year after year, strategists get downplayed. And it's a short trip from downplayed to deprioritized. When strategists are neglected, their marginalization is normalized. Their absence becomes the extent of their presence.

That's why the strategy trap is so insidious. It not only prioritizes strategy over the strategist, but it also makes the strategist seem irrelevant.

The bottom line: Strategy is all about strategy. It breathes its own exhaust.

Strategy has made a career out of ignoring the strategist.[3]

But here's the breakthrough insight: Things don't have to be this way.

THE CHOICE

Each individual and organization has a clear-cut choice to make: Are you going to focus on strategy or strategists?

In choosing strategy, the world remains much the same. And that may be desirable if you're launching one wildly successful strategy after another. But the data suggest otherwise. Research shows a vast majority of strategies fail to achieve their desired results.[4]

What other workflow could fail more often than it succeeds and still hold your organization's perpetual allegiance?

In choosing strategists, the world unfolds in a radically different way. You see strategists as the upstream cause, and you see strategy as the downstream effect. You, therefore, choose to push upstream to focus, first and always, on strategists.

All strategy then flows from there.

In a strategist-driven world, the solution is strikingly simple: The best way to generate more and better strategies is to cultivate more and better strategists. Full stop.

FROM STRATEGY TO STRATEGISTS

In pivoting from strategy to strategists, three truths loom large.

Being pro-strategist doesn't equate to being anti-strategy.
This book isn't anti-strategy—just the opposite.

No strategist can be themselves or do their job without strategy. Strategy is central to who they are, how they operate, and why they matter.

But strategy is forever a means, and never an end.

Strategy's true purpose is to serve strategists, not reign over them. Since the strategy trap refuses to accept this reality, it spends its days trying to sabotage the strategist.

This book, if anything, is anti-strategy trap.

Untapped strategists are everywhere.

Too many organizations claim they can't find enough strategists to promote from the inside or hire from the outside. This alleged drought is a mirage of their own making. Every organization has leaders and followers. And every leader and follower is a potential strategist. They only need to be activated and supported.

In breaking free from strategy's regime, you see that untapped strategists are everywhere—within every organization, every division, every level, every rank, every role, and every pool of prospective hires. It's a story of abundance, not scarcity.

Organizations should ask why they insist on having more creatives on hand to be innovative but fail to question if they have enough strategists on hand to be strategic.

Strategists are starving for support.

The paucity of books, articles, courses, trainings, and investments devoted to strategists is unacceptable. Until strategists have the tools necessary to define reality on their terms, the strategy trap will continue to steal the day.

Organizations would never ask employees to practice accounting without first ensuring their training as accountants. The same holds true for law, finance, data science, engineering, design, audit, cybersecurity, and the like.

That begs the question: Why do organizations ask employees to create and manage strategy without first preparing and supporting them to be strategists?

LIFELONG STRATEGIST

This book is dedicated to making you a lifelong strategist.

It unlocks the insights you need to live this identity into action. Right here. Right now.

You learn the ins and outs of:

Who strategists are.
What strategists believe.
How strategists behave.
Where strategists thrive.
When strategists strike.
Why strategists matter.

This book is built for you and your journey.

The first two chapters show you how to flip the script from strategy to strategists. With the balance of the book, you master the Five Habits, Four Skills, Three Choices, Two Fixes, One Mission, and Zero Doubt that make strategists tick.

Here's an overview:

Chapter 1 defines the essence of the strategist.

Strategists do things by design, not by default. They are disciplined in their deliberateness. For strategists, anticipation is constant. Ownership is contagious. And being effective is everything.

Chapter 2 explains how to avoid the strategy trap.

Strategists live by an enduring truth: Where your attention goes, your results follow. If you start with strategy, you center on a *what*. If you start with strategists, you center on a *who*. The difference? Players win championships. Playbooks don't.

Chapters 3–7 illustrate the *Five Habits* of the strategist.

Strategists lead time. Others manage it. Strategists impose clarity. Others hope for it. Strategists think in questions. Others idolize answers. Strategists push upstream. Others camp downstream. And strategists see around corners. Others mindlessly react to whatever comes next.

Chapters 8–11 spotlight the *Four Skills* of the strategist.

Strategists never miss an opportunity to sharpen their skill set. They are deliberate and disciplined in their desire to continuously improve their craft. To decide better. To message better. To innovate better. And to coach better. They study and practice these four skills again and again until they become a way of life.

Chapters 12–14 delineate the *Three Choices* of the strategist.

Strategists resist the temptation to build the house before the foundation is poured. They keep bringing back the discussion to three fundamental questions: Where are you going to play? When are you going to strike? How are you going to win?

Chapters 15–16 reveal the *Two Fixes* of the strategist.

Strategists reject the artificial certainty of a strategic plan. For them, strategy is a series of bets based on odds, stakes, and contingencies. Strategists also know restricting strategy to the C-suite is a fast way to fail. They believe strategy work must graduate from the precious few to the empowered many.

Chapter 17 details the *One Mission* of the strategist.

Strategists see every situation as an equation. Their job? Solve for strategists. They figure out how, when, and where to get more strategists in the mix. How do you train more strategists? How do you hire more strategists? How do you promote more strategists? How do you place more bets on strategists? How do you make it harder for non-strategists to thrive?

Chapter 18 speaks to the *Zero Doubt* strategists must have in living their identity into action.

Strategy isn't dead. It's simply snared in a trap of its own making. Have zero doubt that strategy needs the strategist to break free from its tired, vain, and ineffective ways. The time to save strategy from itself is long overdue.

Bonus Section: Strategist's Notebook

This book also includes a special feature called the Strategist's Notebook. These bonus ideas deliver a mix of tips and advice on how to be a savvy, well-rounded strategist. The last installment offers more than sixty models and methods you can quickly consult to bolster your strategy work.

THE BEST CURATORS

The best writers are often the best readers. Why?

The best writers know a time-tested truth: iron sharpens iron. By studying the craft of other writers, the best writers make their own writing even better.

Strategists follow a similar path. Trying to think big thoughts while sitting alone and empty-handed is rarely helpful. The best strategists are the best curators.

Strategists comb through countless resources—books, articles, blogs, newsletters, podcasts, case studies, speeches, and interviews—seeking first-rate ideas to adopt or adapt. They use these curated insights to continuously improve the world around them.

This book aims for the same: to build up your library of learnings and un-learnings on how to be a lifelong strategist.

BELIEVE IN THE STRATEGIST

The artist Marcel Duchamp, one of the founders of conceptual art, espoused a core philosophy: "I don't believe in art. I believe in the artist."[5]

For Duchamp, there's no such thing as art without the artist. The former is always already derivative of the latter. Therefore, art can never create better art. Only the artist can do that.

This book advances a similar view.

Strategy has no chance of getting out of its own way to unlock its full potential: only the strategist can do that. Strategy's best future, therefore, hinges on a single, upstream question: Do you have enough strategists at the ready to revolutionize your strategy work?

The time has come to believe anew—to believe bone-deep—in the strategist.

That starts with you.

THE STRATEGIST

This book prioritizes the strategist.

But doing so is all for naught unless the prevailing myths about strategists get debunked. These myths not only reflect but also reinforce the strategy trap's aim to undermine strategists. These fallacies must be exposed and extinguished.

Here's a start.

Myth 1: You need permission to be a strategist.

Strategy wants to operate like a celebrity. Everyone knows its name. No room is off-limits. It forever wants more followers. And it loves restricting access to the party.

But being a strategist is a choice, not a contest. There's no governing body dictating who can or can't be a strategist. No big exam to pass. No special degree to earn. No waiting period to endure. No red velvet rope to negotiate.

Sure, organizations control who has strategy in their title. But they can't dictate who blends strategy into their way of being—no more than they can stop you from being intelligent, ethical, or professional.

If you choose to be a strategist and to live this identity into action, you don't need permission to be you.

Myth 2: Doing strategy work makes you a strategist.

Working on strategy doesn't make you a strategist, just as meditating doesn't make you a monk. Strategizing and meditating are activities. Such activities may alter your routine, but they don't rewire your identity.

Choosing to be a strategist, like being a monk, transforms your identity. And your identity drives your way of being. Every day, every discussion, every decision—you're a strategist. And by saying yes to being a strategist, you're saying no to being a non-strategist.

Having a certain title, degree, or reporting line doesn't make you a strategist, just as the absence of such things doesn't make you a non-strategist.

Strategists are known by their actions, not by their accessories.

Myth 3: Strategists are an endangered species.

The high watermark of irony? Countless organizations insist on having a strategic plan in place, presuming it signals foresight, stability, credibility, and legitimacy. But these same organizations never bother to ask if they have enough strategists at the ready to ensure that the plan is owned and effective.

If anyone tries to convince you strategists are born or rare, don't buy what they are selling. Look for the motivation behind their message: How are they benefitting from peddling this fable of scarcity?

Strategists have never been an endangered species. They are an untapped army—spread across every organization—just waiting to be activated and supported.

Myth 4: Strategists are modern-day generals.

Most authors retrace the etymology of strategy to the Greek word *strategos*. It means "the art of the general." Since CEOs have long been viewed as the modern-day generals of society, this association feeds a common assumption: If you're a CEO, you also must be a master strategist.

To break free from this myth, take another military saying to heart: generals die in bed.

Translation: generals don't die on the battlefield with their soldiers but instead in the calm and comfort of their bed. They repeatedly order their soldiers to risk everything without doing the same.

It's a cautionary tale for everyone involved in strategy work. Don't be so detached from the consequences of your decisions. Strategy can't be the sole purview of detached leaders who never see the front lines.

What battle was ever won with all generals and no army? Strategy must be owned by the entire organization, leaders and followers alike.

Sure, you want your CEO to be a sound strategist. More importantly, you want your CEO to be obsessed with growing more and better strategists at every level of your organization.

Only then will your strategy not die in bed.

Myth 5: Strategists are experts in strategy.

This statement is technically true but intellectually suspect. Yes, strategists know a ton about strategy. But notice what's not being said: that strategists are the makers of strategy.

Great strategy comes from great strategists. There's no other source.

Consider meteorologists by way of comparison. They, too, are experts in their field. Yet they don't produce the weather, the subject of their expertise.

It's a subtle yet significant point. Strategy's failure to acknowledge its cause-and-effect dependency on the strategist is neither accidental nor inconsequential. It's calculated. It's systematic. And it's self-serving. This denial allows strategy to reinforce its messiah complex via a virgin birth.

ON THEIR OWN TERMS

Defining strategists solely by who they aren't only confirms the strategy trap's home-field advantage. It's playing defense to the strategy trap's unrelenting offense. The better approach? Describe strategists on their terms.

No word better captures the essence of the strategist than deliberate.

Strategists are deliberate in who they are, how they think, what they do, and why they matter.

Not always right, strategists are religiously reasoned. They are intentional. They are studied. They are choiceful. And they are next-minded—always striving to anticipate what may or may not come next. Strategists make decisions before decisions make them.

If they have a creed, it's this: Strategists do things by design, not by default.

Strategists are learners. They are driven by a growth mindset. They are curious. Open-minded. Reflective. Interdisciplinary. Ambitious to learn more, to learn better, to learn faster. Strategists believe learning *how* to learn is a superpower.

Strategists are disciplined. They are self-motivated but never self-satisfied. They push for purpose. Feed good habits. Starve bad habits. Create systems. Set boundaries. Edit beliefs. Keep score. Strategists know nothing great can be achieved without first being owned.

Strategists are balanced. They don't traffic in absolutes. There is no perfect strategy, no sure bet for them. They don't subscribe to all-or-nothing thinking. Strategists focus on probabilities. Contingencies. Context. Timing. Tradeoffs. Rethinking. Being less wrong. Strategists work hard not to be prisoners of their own perspective.

Strategists are grounded. They don't buy, sell, or swap drama. They don't gossip. They don't complain. There's no ego. No excuses. Strategists don't hide from themselves. They stay humble and hungry at all times. If they are the smartest person in the room, strategists know they are in the wrong room.

Strategists are practical. They don't argue with reality.[6] They don't waste time trying to prosecute the past, prove they were right, or wish things were different. Strategists accept reality, even if they intensely want to change it.

Strategists are versatile. They get above, below, and beyond any situation. They climb the ladder up to see a balcony view. What's the long-term view of this situation? They dig beneath to structure the unstructured. What foundational clarity is missing? And they see around corners. Why are things trending in this direction? Strategists work not only in your organization but also *on* your organization.

Strategists are farsighted. They play the long game. They are patient and persistent. In their daily work, their mode is more farmer than firefighter. Strategists don't allow what they want now to betray what they want most.

Strategists are savvy. They believe the right facts rarely win the day with the wrong frames. They fight for messages that not only stick but also spread. Revise, rethink, refine, rewrite, and rewrite the rewrites. They don't tolerate confusion or clutter in thought or action. Strategists know strategy is sold, not bought.

Strategists are resilient. They don't get overtaken by events.[7] As things get worse, they get better. They feed the essential by starving the nonessential. Strategists have a knack for converting a crisis into a breakthrough opportunity.

Strategists are coaches. They strive to bring out the best in everyone around them. They know the power of alternating between teaching and learning, enabling each to inspire the other. For strategists, coaching is a calling that can't be ignored.

Strategists are wise. They doubt their ideas, not their identity. And they never find themselves absent of a strategy. Strategists keep the words of futurist Alvin Toffler top of mind: "If you do not develop a strategy of your own, you become a part of someone else's strategy."[8]

ONE QUESTION

Jocko Willink, retired Navy SEAL and bestselling author, believes the totality of leadership boils down to one unavoidable question: Are you effective or ineffective?[9]

If you're ineffective, in Willink's view, the rest is irrelevant.

It's a good way to think about strategists, too. Strategists are, above all, effective.

Anything less is contrary to who they are and why they matter.

STRATEGIST'S NOTEBOOK

WHAT IS STRATEGY?
As a strategist, you'll be asked a basic question of definition: What is strategy?

There's a reason this simple question eludes an easy answer: a standard definition of strategy doesn't exist.

In 2012, two researchers analyzed the field of strategy from 1962 to 2008 and found ninety-one unique definitions of the term strategy.[10] Yes, you read that right: ninety-one different answers to the same question of how to define strategy. And note that this research study ended in 2008.

LACK OF CLARITY AND COHERENCE
That the question of "What is strategy?" lacks an established, accepted response is pure irony because finding an author who fails to mention clarity and coherence as two hallmark features of a good strategy is difficult to do.

So, yes, the two elements considered to be the bedrock of good strategy—clarity and coherence—are precisely the same ones missing from a definition of strategy.

What does this mean for you? You can either adopt an existing definition of strategy that resonates with you or craft your own. Either way, don't take the unwise route of skipping or shortchanging this critical step in your journey.

Case in point: Imagine you've built a brilliant strategy and are pitching it to decision-makers. What if one of them asks you to pause and provide a basic definition of strategy that undergirds your thinking?

Every strategist needs a working definition of strategy—one that's clear enough to stick and flexible enough to evolve.

SAMPLE DEFINITIONS

To assist in developing your own working definition of strategy, below are ten examples. They provide a sense of the diverging and converging concepts at play as you sculpt your own definition of strategy.

> "Strategy explains how an organization, faced with competition, will achieve superior performance."[11]
>
> — MICHAEL PORTER

> "A strategy is a mix of policy and action designed to overcome a significant challenge."[12]
>
> — RICHARD RUMELT

> "Strategy is about shaping the future—it is about how people attain desirable ends with available means."[13]
>
> — MAX MCKEOWN

> "[Strategy is] your plan to compete. It's the bets you're making, your plan of attack to win and achieve your business goals."[14]
>
> — BRAD CHASE

> "Strategy is, in essence, problem-solving, and the best approach depends upon the specific problem at hand. Your environment dictates your approach to strategy."[15]
>
> — MARTIN REEVES, KNUT HAANAES, and JANMEJAYA SINHA

"True strategy is about placing bets and making hard choices. The objective is not to eliminate risk but to increase the odds of success."[16]

- ROGER MARTIN

"The strategy sets the framework within which future decisions will be made, but at the same time it leaves room for learning from ongoing developments and for discretion to act based on what is learned."[17]

- TIM LUEHRMAN

"Strategy is a deliberate search for a plan of action that will develop a business's competitive advantage and compound it."[18]

- BRUCE HENDERSON

"Strategy is a diagnosis that defines or explains a business challenge or opportunity, a decision or set of decisions for dealing with the challenge or opportunity, and a coherent set of actions to deliver on the decisions so as to create sustainable advantage and superior returns."[19]

- GREG FISHER, JOHN WISNESKI,
and RENE BAKKER

"[S]trategy is revolution; everything else is tactics."[20]

- GARY HAMEL

YOUR DEFINITION
Which definitions resonate with you? A helpful exercise is to craft your definition of strategy now and

revisit your words after reading this book. What changed? What stayed the same?

For more ways to describe strategy, the book *Strategy Safari: A Guided Tour Through the Wilds of Strategic Management* by Henry Mintzberg, Bruce Ahlstrand, and Joseph Lampel is a good resource.[21] The authors outline ten schools of thought related to strategy. They argue for a multidimensional definition of strategy that includes five parts: 1) strategy as a plan, 2) strategy as a pattern, 3) strategy as a position, 4) strategy as a perspective, and 5) strategy as a ploy.[22]

As you reflect on the various definitions above, it's worth underscoring the obvious: none of these definitions of strategy say a single word about strategists.

That's the subtle yet seismic impact of the strategy trap. Strategists are nowhere to be found in strategy's profile.

THE NAME GAME

Many self-appointed strategy experts play a game that deserves to be disrupted. They ask a room full of people to provide their definition of strategy.

Then they spend a dizzying amount of time ridiculing the answers, saying: "You're defining a vision, not strategy; you're defining goals, not strategy; you're defining objectives, not strategy; you're defining actions, not strategy."

How should you respond? Before shifting the focus from strategy to strategists, take a moment to complicate this supposed chasm between strategy and vision/goals/objectives/actions.

You: What's the secret sauce behind crafting a great vision?

Expert: You need to…

You: That sounds like a decidedly strategic approach.

Expert: Yes, very much so.

You: Well, don't these strategic choices constitute a strategy?

Expert: Huh?

You: Behind every great vision is a set of forecasts, bets, and choices. That's strategy.

You: It takes a great strategy to build a great vision.

You: The same logic holds true for goals, objectives, and actions.

Expert: What are you saying exactly?

You: Strategy already lives inside these concepts.

If the expert becomes defensive, get ready for a retreat to their résumé. They may drop the names of great companies that have paid for their strategy services. They may highlight how many strategic plans they have developed during their career. They may even point to books or articles they have penned on strategy.

There's no reason to doubt or disparage any of these accomplishments.

Simply ask a reframing question: Do you feel you have activated, trained, and supported enough strategists over the course of your career?

THE STRATEGY TRAP

You've chosen to be a lifelong strategist. Now what? Conquering the strategy trap is job one for every strategist. Recall that strategy operates by prioritizing strategy and deprioritizing the strategist. Since it happens with such ease and regularity, the strategy trap can be hard to detect— and even harder to defeat.

Beating the strategy trap starts with two steps: recognize and rethink.

RECOGNIZE

The strategy trap must be spotted before it can be stopped. How can you tell if you or your organization are caught in the strategy trap? Review your record.

Have you had strategies that flat-out failed? Have you had strategies that were long on promises but short on results? Have you had strategies that were good but not great? If so, the strategy trap is likely at play.

Three subpar strategies are common to the strategy trap: fizzle, orphan, and fragile. Think of them as the FOF zone.

> **Fizzle strategies** start with great fanfare. But instead of strengthening over time, they weaken and eventually wash out due to a lack of sustained progress. They quietly migrate from the desk to the shelf to the storage closet.
>
> **Orphan strategies** are crafted entirely by the C-suite. Since only a few top-level leaders create these strat-

egies, they fail to get adopted by the rest of the organization. High on lip service and low on elbow grease, orphan strategies devour lots of attention but deliver little impact.

Fragile strategies look sound on paper but collapse in practice. They are too stiff to bend, too slow to pivot, and too sure to self-correct. They can't survive the inevitable setbacks that come with an ever-changing environment.

What's missing from the FOF zone? Ownership. The kind that pulses throughout the entire organization in all directions.

If owned, strategies get stronger over time. *They don't fizzle.*

If owned, strategies get adopted at every level. *They aren't orphaned.*

If owned, strategies bend but never break. *They are anti-fragile.*

Ownership comes from having strategists positioned at all levels of your organization. If your strategies lack ownership, your organization lacks enough strategists. And if you lack enough strategists, your organization will be forever stuck in the strategy trap.

RETHINK

Beyond recognizing the strategy trap, you must know how to defeat it.

The key is to rethink strategy's nature. Strategy's history is a master class in marginalizing the strategist. Year after year, a parade of books, articles, and videos on strategy are put out that say practically nothing about strategists.

Case in point: A few years back, *Harvard Business Review* curated its top ten strategy articles of all time and converted them into a book.[23] What term is absent from every single title? Strategist. This same glaring omission is replicated in the leading textbook on strategy, now in its twelfth edition, *Exploring Strategy: Text and Cases*.[24]

To rethink strategy and to upend the strategy trap, you must pursue three pivots:

Object → Identity

Part-time → Full-time

Finite → Infinite

FROM OBJECT TO IDENTITY

A tool in your tool kit. A skill on your résumé. A plan for your organization. Notice the common thread in these standard descriptions of strategy? Strategy is defined as an object.

Viewing strategy as an object only reinforces a sense of otherness—strategy is a thing that lives outside of you. It's how strategy becomes externalized and episodic.

You perform strategy work on some days but not others. You think strategically in some situations but not all. Some team members work on strategy, but others don't. Your organization has a strategic plan in some years but not others.

Viewed as an object, strategy is rented rather than owned.

To rethink strategy, you must redefine it. Strategy can no longer be a what—a tool, skill, or plan. Strategy must be a who—the core of your identity.

It takes no less than an existential shift from It-ness to I-ness to see strategy as an extension of you. More than what you do, strategy is who you are. It propels your way of being.

Once you choose to be a strategist, your mindset, beliefs, and habits not only reflect but also reinforce this identity. And not on some days and in some ways, but always and in all ways—so much so that you feel awry when you behave in nonstrategic ways.

Viewed as an identity, strategy is owned rather than rented.

Redefining strategy from a *what* to a *who* is similar to cultivating a good habit. James Clear, a leading strategist on the study of habit formation, contends most people fail to cement good habits because they try changing the wrong thing.[25]

They focus on the desired outcome they want to achieve: the *what*. Then they turn their attention to the process of achieving it: the *how*. While both elements are important to habit change, neither prompts you to edit your identity: the *who*.

For Clear, upgrading your who is *the* best way to make a good habit stick: "The ultimate form of intrinsic motivation is when a habit becomes part of your identity. It's one thing to say I'm the type of person who *wants* this. It's something very different to say I'm the type of person who *is* this."[26]

Clear continues, "After all, when your behavior and your identity are fully aligned, you are no longer pursuing behavior change. You are simply acting like the type of person you already believe yourself to be."[27]

Clear's theory suggests why the strategy trap is so deceptively effective. Talk of the what or how of strategy rarely focuses on the who of strategy. So, if you start by centering on strategy, you typically stay and end with strategy. And the strategist remains a footnote, at best, along the way.

By contrast, if you start by prioritizing the strategist, you remain focused on the strategist—and on fully aligning your identity and your behavior. At this point, owning strategy is a natural and necessary expression of your identity. After all, if you identify as a strategist, you can't rent strategy and still remain true to your being. You must own it.

The key to defeating the strategy trap is to focus, first and always, on the who of strategy, not on the what or how of strategy.

FROM PART-TIME TO FULL-TIME

Another way to rethink strategy is to recalibrate it from a part-time engagement to a full-time calling. How so? Take your lead from the entrepreneur.

Entrepreneurs don't spend their days sitting around talking about entrepreneurship. They don't behave like an entrepreneur on some days but not on others. They don't limit their entrepreneurial work to off-site retreats. They don't allow themselves or their organizations to operate in non-entrepreneurial ways.

They spend every waking hour *being* an entrepreneur.

For them, entrepreneurship is never an abstract concept. Being an entrepreneur is a way of life. It drives every aspect of who they are, what they do, and why they matter. And not only for them but also for everyone around them.

If you are or know an entrepreneur, you can attest to a simple truth: There's no off switch to them and their identity. They are entrepreneurs, always and in all ways.

Taking a step back, the bigger picture comes into focus: entrepreneurship is built on a who, not a what.

This same identity-driven clarity must hold true for the strategist.

It's not enough to talk about strategy. Not enough to think strategically. Not enough to have strategy listed on your résumé or included in your title. Not enough to be involved in strategy work at off-site retreats. Not enough to allow some individuals to do strategy work while the rest of your team watches on the sidelines.

The time has come for the strategist to be like the entrepreneur: all in.

It's time to make strategy the core of your identity. Time to make it structure and drive everything else. Time to glue down the "ON" switch. Time to be a strategist, always and in all ways.

Yet it only happens if you rebuild strategy, like entrepreneurship, on a who, not a what.

COMMITTED vs. INVOLVED

Chicken: "Hey, Pig, we should open a restaurant."

Pig: "What would we call it?"

Chicken: "Ham-n-Eggs."

Pig: "No thanks. I'd be committed. You'd only be involved."

FROM FINITE TO INFINITE

The third way to rethink strategy is to reposition its horizon. The strategist Simon Sinek believes life boils down to two types of games: finite and infinite.[28]

Finite games are bound by fixed rules. They also have set finish lines. Given these conditions, finite players adopt a win-or-lose mentality.

And since everybody wants to win, and nobody can stand to lose, it's easy to overvalue such things as short-term thinking, near-term results, and zero-sum perspectives in a finite context. Sports are a prime example of a finite pursuit.

Infinite games, according to Sinek, reflect infinite possibilities. They have no fixed customs and no predetermined ends. Given these conditions, infinite players adopt an expansive mindset that places a premium on openness, flexibility, and farsightedness.

Nor do infinite players get bogged down in the binary logic of winning or losing.

They instead focus on playing the game to the best of their ability, striving to get better every step of the way, and leaving their surroundings better than they found them. Unlike finite players—who see only the starts, stops, and sprints of the game—infinite players fully embrace the journey.

Sinek believes business, like most of life, is an infinite game. But he thinks too many leaders, overly consumed by competition, try to play this infinite game with a finite mentality.

This misalignment feeds a series of unwise behaviors. For instance, these misguided leaders prioritize profits over people. They allow short-term gains to supersede long-term viability. And they neglect to see how their insatiable desire to win can create the ideal conditions to trigger their eventual decline or demise.

Sinek explains how Microsoft, Apple, and Walmart thrived under the infinite thinking of Bill Gates, Steve Jobs, and Sam Walton yet struggled under the finite leadership of Steve Ballmer, John Sculley, and Mike Duke.

Sinek's notion of finite and infinite games is a useful analogy for understanding the strategy trap.

Strategies = finite games.

✓ They are bound to fixed plans.

✓ They adhere to set finish lines.

✓ They tend to be preoccupied with winning.

✓ And they come and go at a dizzying rate, given their mixed performance.

Strategists = the infinite game.

✓ They are farsighted, not shortsighted.

✓ They use rules as tools, not decrees.

✓ They are adaptive, not prescriptive.

✓ They are leaders and followers, not winners and losers.

✓ And they steward your organization's mission, vision, and values for decades on end.

Since the strategy trap is all about strategy, it keeps you locked into playing an endless cycle of finite games. Worse still, if your strategy falters or fails, you are conditioned to believe the solution is to produce yet another strategy. And another one after that, over and over again.

But the cure is nothing more than a perpetuation of the disease. Strategy can't fix strategy. Only strategists can create the type of ownership that strategy needs to thrive.

In choosing to play the infinite game, you rethink strategy. You focus on the infinite nature of strategists, not the finite nature of strategy.

The strategy trap is no match for the infinite mindset.

FLIP THE SCRIPT

As the saying goes, "Nobody joins a cult. They just postpone the decision to leave." The same goes for the strategy trap. Individuals and organizations don't join the trap as much as they fail to take the necessary steps to avoid or escape it.

Make no mistake: defeating the strategy trap is the most important step on the strategist's journey. Start by recognizing the trap's reach as well as its resistance to change. Then rethink how strategy manages to cast itself as the main character in every story.

Flip the script. Carve clarity into the fact that strategy lives downstream from the strategist. Therefore, any thoughtful engagement with strategy must start upstream—at the headwaters—with the strategist.

Strategists first. Strategists first. Strategists first.

STRATEGIST'S NOTEBOOK

WHAT IS EXECUTION?

The term execution, like strategy, lacks a standard definition. It, therefore, suffers from the same inkblot ailment: plenty of interpretations, not much consensus.

As a strategist, you must be equally committed to execution as you are to strategy.

While that's easy to say on paper, it's difficult to deliver in practice. A PwC survey of executives finds only 8 percent consider their top leaders "very effective" in both strategy and execution.[30] That's less than one in ten top leaders who can be trusted to advance both priorities well for their respective organizations.

As you craft your own approach to execution, here's a sampling of ideas and insights to consider.

FALSE DICHOTOMY

The strategist Roger Martin finds the common definition of execution to be "fundamentally unhelpful" because it perpetuates a false dichotomybetween strategy and execution.[31] It suggests strategy is the cerebral stuff happening at the top of the organization, where choices are made, and execution is the blue-collar work occurring down below, where those choices are obeyed.

Martin rejects this framing because he believes choices—what to do and what not to do—are made at every level in both strategy and execution.[32] Choices are choices, independent of whether you label them strategy choices or execution choices.

IDEAS & INSIGHTS

Graham Kenny claims the biggest challenge to execution is effectively translating "broad ideas about what makes you competitive at the organizational level into concrete actions for progress at the individual level."[33] To bridge this gap, Kenny recommends five rules:

1) Narrow your focus.

2) Make the statements imperative.

3) Give the statements real owners.

4) Separate out your strategy meetings.

5) Appoint a monitor.[34]

Rosabeth Moss Kanter believes the best way to disrupt conventional thinking is to focus on execution first and strategy second.[35] She likens strategy and execution to improvisational theater: "A strategy takes shape from what actors do in front of audiences that provide feedback."[36] Before announcing your strategy in a big way, Kanter suggests getting feedback on your execution, adapting your thinking, and then building momentum so that you launch your vision with a tailwind.[37] To pursue this approach, Kanter proposes four steps:

1) Question everything.

2) Inform everyone, then empower champions.

3) Keep relationships tight and rules loose.

4) Modify quickly.[38]

Michael Mankins asserts the "plan-then-do" approach to strategy and execution is not only obslete, but also dangerous, insofar as it can't respond fast or smart enough to your ever-changing environment.[39] He advocates replacing it with a "decide-do/ refine-do" approach built on five pillars:

1) Treat strategy as evergreen.

2) Value flexibility.

3) Think of strategy as a portfolio of options, not bonds.

4) Create response mechanisms.

5) Test and learn, then test some more.[40]

In *Strategy That Works: How Winning Companies Close the Strategy-to-Execution Gap,* Paul Leinwand and Cesare Mainardi view capabilities as the essential link between strategy and execution.[41] For them, winning organizations fully integrate capabilities, strategy, and execution. To create this coherence, they point to five acts of unconventional leadership:

1) Commit to an identity.

2) Translate the strategic into the everyday.

3) Put your culture to work.

4) Cut costs to grow stronger.

5) Shape your future.[42]

Simon Horan and Michael Connerty believe results suffer when organizations fail to balance the inherent tensions between strategy and execution. They maintain leaders must balance four core tensions to close the gap between strategy and execution:

1) An inspiring end-state vs. challenging targets.

2) Top-down control vs. democratization of change.

3) Capability development vs. pressure for results.

4) Creativity vs. discipline.[43]

Ricardo Viana Vargas and Edivandro Conforto researched the gap between strategy and execution.[44] For them, bridging the divide involves answering ten key questions:

1) Is delivery as important to you as design?

2) Does the leadership team take responsibility for delivery, too?

3) Do you mobilize the right resources?

4) Do you leverage insights on customers and competitors?

5) Is your implementation bold, focused, and as simple as possible?

6) Do you promote team engagement and cross-business collaboration?

7) Do you own the decisions you make?

8) Do you check ongoing initiatives before committing to new ones?

9) Do you develop robust plans but allow for missteps?

10) Do you celebrate success and recognize those who have done good work?[45]

Gary Neilson, Karla Martin, and Elizabeth Powers study organizations with a proven record of successful strategy implementation.[46] They claim the best organizations share a common set of traits, such as:

1) Everyone has a good idea of the decision and actions for which he or she is responsible.

2) Important information about the competitive environment gets to headquarters quickly.

3) Once made, decisions are rarely second-guessed.

4) Information flows freely across organizational boundaries.

5) Field and line employees usually have the information they need to understand the bottom-line impact of their day-to-day choices.[47]

One of the most well-known books on execution is by Larry Bossidy and Ram Charan.[48] Execution is doomed, argue Bossidy and Charan, unless it's driven by three core processes: people, strategy, and operations.

If you don't have the right people in the right place, your execution will suffer. If your strategy doesn't prefigure execution into its formation, your execution will fail. If your operations aren't fully aligned with your people process and your strategy process, your execution will collapse.

Another insight worth remembering is James Clear's observation that winners and losers aspire to the exact same goal.[49] The difference in the outcome comes down to execution.

COMMON THEMES
When executing on execution, there is no standard approach. Nevertheless, you can see some common themes emerge around focus, flexibility, accountability, and alignment.

FOCUS	How can your organization sharpen its focus to attack only the essential elements of your execution agenda?
FLEXIBILITY	Since execustion is more fluid than fixed, how can your organization become smarter and faster in adapting to change and feedback?
ACCOUNTABILITY	How can your organization make execution the responsibility of everyone involved, all the time, including top leadership?
ALIGNMENT	How can your organization link people, capabilities, strategy, and operations in more synchronized ways?

As a strategist, you can't allow any daylight between your strategy and your execution. The former must prefigure the latter. And the latter must steadily refine the former. Taken together, each must rely on the other for its vitality and durability.

Just as creating more and better strategies comes from having more and better strategists, the same holds true for execution. Driving more and better execution comes from having more and better strategists at every level of your organization.

5 HABITS

Lead Time
Impose Clarity
Think in Questions
Push Upstream
See around Corners

LEAD TIME

More than five hundred managers at twenty-five companies were asked to identify the biggest obstacles keeping them from being more strategic.[50] Guess what challenge ranked first and was cited by 96 percent of respondents? Time.

If you want a surefire way to distinguish a strategist from a non-strategist, examine their relationship to time. Non-strategists manage time; strategists lead time. And the difference is staggering when it comes to carving out space to strategize.

Making a wholesale shift from time management to time leadership is the first habit every strategist must master. And doing so requires you to unlearn your typical schedule.

YOUR DAY IS THEIR TIME

How much of your day is devoted to meetings?

One study reveals the average leader spends twenty-three hours a week in meetings.[51] (Incidentally, over the course of a forty-five-year career, this rate translates to twenty-two years of meetings.) This number would be great news if these meetings were strategic in content or consequence. Sadly, most are the opposite of strategic.

How much of your day is consumed by email?

Research suggests roughly 306 billion emails are exchanged each day worldwide.[52] The average professional worker receives more than 120 messages daily and spends 28 percent of their workday managing their inbox.[53]

How much of your day deals with drama and conflict?

One study reveals workers spend an average of 2.8 hours a week managing work-related conflicts.[54]

Given the averages above, you devote 276 minutes to meetings, 132 minutes to email, and 33 minutes to conflicts each day. Presuming an 8-hour workday, that leaves you with only 39 minutes left to utilize.

But what about your other time commitments?

That long to-do list? That unexpected but urgent assignment? That personnel issue that needs immediate attention? That special report your boss's boss needs?

It's not a stretch to presume these other activities—along with lunch, a few bathroom breaks, typical interruptions, and checking your phone—consume another twenty minutes of your day.

If so, that leaves you with a mere nineteen minutes of unscheduled time each day. Worse still, these precious few minutes are likely distributed unevenly throughout your day—three minutes here, five minutes there, and so on.

YOUR DAY/THEIR TIME	
Start of the Day	*480 minutes*
Meetings	*-276 minutes*
Emails	*-132 minutes*
Managing Conflicts	*-33 minutes*
Other Items	*-20 minutes*
BALANCE	**19 minutes**

What's missing from your average day? Yes, you guessed it: sizable blocks of uninterrupted time for you to be deliberate in your thinking and doing.

Time to ask uncommon questions.

Time to move upstream to focus on sources, not symptoms.

Time to fight for that new level of clarity.

Time to see around corners.

Time to read.

Time to learn.

Time to write and rewrite.

Time, above all, to be a strategist.

DEEP WORK

Strategy work is downright demanding.

It involves different levels of observation: macro and micro, cultural and organizational, team and individual, and theory and practice. It involves different degrees of discerning: known knowns, known unknowns, unknown knowns, and unknown unknowns. It involves different modes of thinking: critical, creative, analytical, reflective, anticipatory, and systems. And finally, it involves different types of doing: listening, questioning, forecasting, forming, framing, and executing.

None of that is shallow work. It's the exact opposite—deep, complex, and consequential.

Strategists know deep work requires total focus and unbroken concentration.

For individuals, a good primer on deep work is Cal Newport's *Deep Work: Rules for Focused Success in a Distracted World*.[55] For organizations, a helpful read is *The 4 Disciplines of Execution* by Chris McChesney, Sean Covey, and Jim Huling.[56]

The latter work recommends four steps (which Newport also adopts) for building a deep-work environment: 1) focus on the wildly important, 2) act on the lead measures,

3) keep a compelling scorecard, and 4) create a cadence of accountability.[57]

The strategist Jim Collins is a firm believer in deep work, though he calls it his "creative time."[58] Collins divides his life into three blocks: 50 percent creative time, 30 percent teaching time, and 20 percent other stuff. Creative time is when Collins not only unlocks his greatest intellectual potential but also produces his most meaningful results.

Collins translates his percentage goal for creative time into an hourly target: he must complete one thousand hours of creative work per year. To hold himself accountable, Collins records a breakdown of his hours at the end of each day. He also tracks his monthly progress on a whiteboard in his office for others to see.

Sure, this sounds like a good model in theory. But does it actually work in practice, and is it sustainable? Collins's record of success speaks for itself. He hasn't missed his one-thousand-hour annual goal in more than thirty years. Yes, that's three consecutive decades of deep work.

Little surprise that one of Collins's favorite quotes comes from the novelist Gustave Flaubert: "Be regular and orderly in your life, so that you may be violent and original in your work."[59]

Lest you think deep work is a luxury only monks, philosophers, or artists can afford, consider this statement from former Secretary of Defense James Mattis: "If I was to sum up the single biggest problem of senior leadership in the Information Age, it's a lack of reflection.... We need solitude to refocus on prospective decision-making, rather than just reacting to problems as they arise."[60]

In short, if your day—and, by extension, your week, month, and year—lacks big chunks of uninterrupted time for deep work, you are managing time rather than leading it.

And no strategist can be their best if they work in such shallow surroundings.

LEADING TIME

A great primer on the mechanics of time leadership is Greg McKeown's book *Essentialism: The Disciplined Pursuit of Less*.[61] McKeown runs every decision through a highly selective filter: Is this proposed activity essential or nonessential?

Essential activities constitute the wisest investment of your time, energy, and attention. They should be pursued. Nonessential activities represent all the rest. They should be ignored.

Filtering your world in this highly structured way, you soon realize how many nonessential activities consume a typical day.

Start by dispensing with anything that looks or sounds like drama. Keep repeating the Polish proverb: "Not my circus. Not my monkeys."

Next comes the seemingly important stuff. Important for whom? Important why? Important how? Important when?

The question isn't whether it matters; it's whether it matters most for you—and only you—at this precise moment.

Your singular purpose is to zero in on what you consider to be the highest and best use of your time. McKeown calls it doing the right thing in the right way at the right time.[62]

Time leadership involves saying yes to the right things and no to all, not some, of the rest.

Doing so takes clarity, courage, and diplomacy. And McKeown's work provides a compelling framework and vocabulary to do just that. His most notable line is worth repeating: "Our highest priority is to protect our ability to prioritize."[63]

A similar line of logic has been attributed to Warren Buffett. His strategy for prioritization runs as follows: Create a list of your top twenty-five goals. Identify the five goals that matter most. Then take the twenty remaining goals and work hard to avoid them. Why? Because those twenty goals will keep you from achieving your top five. In other words, you must prioritize your priorities to see game-changing results.

DEEP-WORK DAY

One concrete way to lead time is to establish a deep-work day. The concept is so simple, it seems nearly impossible to do: Devote one day a week to doing things differently.

No meetings. No emails. No calls. No conflicts. And absolutely no interruptions or distractions. It's just you and your best-thinking self in a state of total focus and unbroken concentration. Pick an essential trend, theme, or problem in your world and spend a full eight hours attacking it like your organization's future depends on it.

Early on, those around you may view deep-work days as nice but unnecessary. Resist the noise. Be disciplined. Stay the course. Soon enough, you will see a stark difference in the quality of your intellectual output.

Your regular days are filled with 1x and 2x ideas—ones that keep things running along a predictable path. And, yes, this type of stability is important to any organization. But your deep-work days can yield 10x ideas and insights—ones that have the potential to unlock breakthrough results for you and your organization.

Similar to the notion of return on investment (ROI), it's worth tracking your return on time (ROT). If a single deep-work day is worth up to ten regular workdays in terms of intellectual output, why would you allow anyone or anything to stand in the way? Once you start protecting your deep-work days at all costs, you are well on your way to leading time.

If creating a deep-work day every week proves impossible, start with two days a month. If that fails, reread McKeown's book and attack your schedule with an essentialist mindset.

What if your boss schedules over your deep-work day with their priority? Follow Neil Pasricha's steadfast rule: A deep-work day can be moved on your calendar but never deleted.[64]

Waiting to find the perfect time to implement a deep-work day is tempting but futile. It's reminiscent of the quip: You plan to read a book on time management just as soon as you can find a place to wedge it into your busy schedule.

Jim Collins describes this rupture in the traditional flow of time as follows: "Think of it as like putting down rocks in the river; if you wait for the river to stop flowing before you walk out and put a rock down, you'll never get one out there."[65] Collins continues, "Instead, better to drop a rock in the flow and make the river go around it."[66]

Drop a deep-think day into your calendar and let the river of activities go around it.

John Donahoe, CEO of Nike, is a true believer in deep-work days. As Donahoe details, "My thinking days give me a refreshed, comprehensive view of how I am spending my time and allow me to recalibrate and adjust my goals, my priorities, and my calendar."[67]

READING REGIMEN

Another way to test whether you're leading time is to track how many hours you devote to reading and learning each week.

Bill Gates created the time to read one book a week during his career at Microsoft.[68] (Gates also took a week-long reading vacation twice a year.) Barack Obama carved out the time to read one hour a day while serving as president of the United States. And Warren Buffett claims he spends 80 percent of his workday reading and thinking.

How did three of the busiest, most accomplished strategists of the modern era devote at least five hours a week to reading and learning? Each of them found a way to pivot from time management to time leadership. If they can do it, why can't you?

Strategists know time is their most valuable asset. If you don't have sound strategies for optimizing your time, you have no chance of reaching your full potential.

STRATEGIST'S NOTEBOOK

#MONKEYFIRST

Did you know Google has a moonshot factory? The organization is called X, and it's located less than two miles from the Googleplex in Mountain View.

As one reporter observes, X doesn't want to improve Google's current portfolio as much as it wants to create the *next* Google.[69]

At X, each moonshot idea must adhere to three principles: tackles a huge problem, proposes a radical solution, and employs workable technology.[70]

Given these ambitious criteria, it's no surprise that the X team finds themselves working on head-scratching projects. Faced with such rich complexity and long odds, it can be difficult for these teams to know where and how to start a project.

Astro Teller, the leader of X and commonly known as the captain of moonshots, advises his teams to start their work with the #MonkeyFirst test. This concept derives from a fictional company that's charged with a seemingly impossible challenge: get a monkey to stand on a tall pedestal and recite Shakespeare.

When most teams are assigned this thought experiment, explains Teller, they believe their first step should be to build the tall pedestal. Why? Compared to training a monkey to speak in the bard's words, building a pedestal seems simple to understand and easy to accomplish. Plus, you can show a completed pedestal to a supervisor or investor in a reasonable time frame to demonstrate progress on the overall project.

But Teller teaches his teams to do the opposite.

X teams focus on the seemingly impossible task first. Namely, they try to figure out how to get a monkey to quote Shakespeare. In Teller's words, "You can always build the pedestal. All of the risk and the learning comes from the extremely hard work of first training the monkey."[71]

Put differently, if you can't find a way to get a monkey to quote Macbeth, there's no need to build the pedestal in the first place. In practical terms, the #MonkeyFirst mantra is shorthand for teams to do the hardest thing first.

Teller's logic seems counterintuitive because most organizations condition their teams to do the easiest thing first. The metaphors sound like this: pick the low-hanging fruit, rack up the quick wins, or follow the path of least resistance.

Most strategy work subscribes to this easiest-thing-first assumption. But Teller's allegory forces you to rethink this popular approach.

If your strategy hinges on a hard solution, and you discover there's no chance of delivering this outcome from the outset, why spend precious time, resources, and opportunity costs completing the easier parts of the strategy? In other words, since your strategy stands or falls on its hardest part, why not start there to determine its overall feasibility?

The #MonkeyFirst mantra also raises a bigger question for organizations: If your strategy is all pedestal and no talking monkey, is it unique and bold enough to pursue in the first place?

This last question speaks to X's core philosophy on problem-solving. They want to tackle intractable problems that produce 10x impact, not 10 percent improvement.

Teller defines the difference between 1,000 percent and 10 percent as follows: "...if you choose to make something 10 percent better, you are almost by definition signing up for the status quo—and trying to make it a little bit better.... But if you sign up for moonshot thinking, if you sign up to make something 10x better, there is no chance of doing that with existing assumptions. You're going to have to throw out the rule book."[72]

Is your strategy signing you up for more of the status quo, or is it enabling you to toss out the rule book and unlock breakthrough results?

IMPOSE CLARITY

Ever heard Jeff Bezos described as a sloppy thinker? Ever seen Bill Gates fail to explain the big picture behind his point? Ever learn of an Apple employee who was unsure of Steve Jobs's expectations for simplicity?

Three stellar strategists. One common denominator: clarity.

Clarity is everything. If doubtful, create a list of successful strategies defined by muddy ideas. Better still, assemble a roster of accomplished strategists known for unclear thinking.

Both tasks prove futile because a sound strategy must necessarily be a clear strategy. The same goes for strategists. A sound strategist must necessarily be a clear-thinking strategist.

Strategists crave clarity. They can't survive without it. So, they fight for it.

They drive the unclear into a corner and force it to surrender. They speak up when something is confusing. They speak out when assumptions go untested. And they refuse to let complexity get its way.

Strategists don't hope for clarity—they impose it. They insist on rethinking, rewriting, and refining until sharpness shines through. Their bias for the simple, the succinct, and the spelled out is unmistakable.

The best organizations are built on clarity. At the deepest level, they understand precisely who they are, what they do, what they don't do, and why they matter. This clearness emanates outward, so everyone else understands it too.

Disney and customer service.
Apple and superior design.
Walmart and saving money.
Harvard and excellence.
Pixar and creativity.
Ikea and affordable design.

Each organization cuts a clear path from its identity to your understanding. Consider the opposite: Can you name an organization excelling at a high level that lacks clarity regarding who they are, what they do, what they don't do, and why they matter?

Strategists know this type of organizational clarity starts with individual clarity.

INDIVIDUAL CLARITY

One of the best ways to create individual clarity is to think about your thinking.

What mental models are you using? What models are you missing? Which model works best in which setting? In asking such questions, know this: there's no perfect way to think about thinking. No single mental model trumps the rest. If anything, you want to have and hone as many mental models as you can manage.

Mental models force you to structure your thinking in deliberate ways. This structure provides the scaffolding to organize your ideas. Organization helps with coherency. Coherency leads to simplicity. And simplicity is the calling card for clarity.

Here's a sample of mental models to use in your efforts to impose clarity:

MENTAL MODEL	DESCRIPTION
First-Principles Thinking	Deconstruct a complex issue by stripping away its assumptions until you reach the basic, irreducible ideas. Use these core truths to establish a new foundation for your knowledge build.
Second-Order Thinking	A cause produces an effect. Most see the impact of a first-order effect and stop there. Second-order thinking focuses on the effects of the effect, the second-order implications of the first-order impact. It's similar to identifying the benefit of the benefit.
Convergent & Divergent Thinking	Convergent thinking is critical, analytical, and judgmental. Divergent thinking is creative, intuitive, and nonjudgmental. The key is to allow each mode to flourish on its own without being sabotaged by the other because trying to do both at the same time is "like trying to drive with one foot on the gas and one foot on the brake."[73]
Inversion Thinking	Flip an idea or argument upside down to see it anew from radically different vantage points. Ask: What if the opposite were true? Or take a "why" answer and subject it to a "why not" question.

Analogical Thinking	Apply the characteristics of a familiar situation to an unfamiliar situation to make the latter more relatable and discernable. Analogical thinking occurs when a company is described as being the Airbnb of this industry or the Tesla of that industry.
Nonlinear Thinking	Linear thinking moves in one direction in a sequential, orderly fashion. Nonlinear thinking is more abstract, originating from various sources, moving in multiple directions, and connecting seemingly unrelated parts. There's no predefined path or logical order to nonlinear thinking.
Abstract Thinking	Take a concrete issue or problem and make it more abstract. If this issue were a shape, what would it be and why? A smell? A place? A public figure? A candy? A song? The goal is to decamp from literal and linear ways of thinking.
If/Then Thinking	Anticipate the effect of an event or action by using an if/then scenario to predict a possible outcome. If this (fill in a cause) happens, you can expect that (fill in an effect) will follow. Scenario-based planning is predicated on if/then thinking.

Counterfactual Thinking	Identify a factual event and imagine how things could have unfolded differently had other choices and conditions led to alternative endings. Downward counterfactual thinking considers how things could have been worse than the current reality. Upward counterfactual thinking assesses how things could have been better.
Integrative Thinking	Faced with opposing ideas, don't settle for an either/or solution. Keep the whole in mind. Test the tension between the concepts. What variables are missing? Think of both/and possibilities rather than either/or choices. Forge a new integrated solution based on the best elements of the component parts.
Systems Thinking	Elevate your view of a situation above the separate pieces, tactics, boundaries, and silos to see a holistic picture of how things work at multiple levels and in various ways. Think in terms of an ecosystem and how the individual parts relate to the collective whole.

Another way to cultivate clear thinking is to guard against unclear thinking. Cognitive biases are systematic errors in your thinking. If left unchecked, they can wreak havoc on your strategy work. The list of cognitive biases is long and continues to grow.

The best place to spend your time is studying Daniel Kahneman's work, starting with his seminal book *Thinking, Fast and Slow*.[74] No other thinker has a better handle on the unclear thinking born of biases than Kahneman.

In naming and taming the cognitive glitches that dominate daily thinking, the aim is to get smarter by being less dumb. Charlie Munger, vice chairman of Berkshire Hathaway, confirms as much when he admits, "It is remarkable how much long-term advantage people like us have gotten by trying to be consistently not stupid, instead of trying to be very intelligent."[75]

ORGANIZATIONAL CLARITY

With individual clarity in place, it's time to turn your attention to organizational clarity.

Patrick Lencioni believes great organizations are led by great leaders who perform three rituals over and over again.[76] First, they create clarity. Second, they overcommunicate clarity. Third, they reinforce clarity.

To create clarity, Lencioni recommends having your organization answer six critical questions: Why do we exist? How do we behave? What do we do? How will we succeed? What is most important right now? Who must do what?[77]

To overcommunicate clarity, Lencioni suggests repeating your answers to these six critical questions at least seven times broadly across your organization. The strategist Roger Martin says it more bluntly: "My experience is that you must explain your choices and the reasoning behind them so many times that you will want to throw up when you hear yourself explain it again—only then will you have done a good job."[78]

To reinforce clarity, Lencioni proposes weaving the six answers to the questions above into the fabric of your organization via its structures, policies, and practices. For Lencioni, there's no such thing as overcommunication when it comes to reinforcing clarity.[79] His advice is to view your role as spreading true rumors.

THE POWER OF NARRATIVE

Whether creating individual clarity or organizational clarity, the best tool to use is the written word. Putting pen to paper is a remarkably clarifying exercise. Just ask Amazon.

You know of Jeff Bezos's longstanding ban on Power Point slides.[80] He insists meetings start by having everyone sit silently and read a narratively structured six-page memorandum on the topic at hand. Following this exercise, which Bezos affectionately refers to as study hall, the group then debates the merits of the written memo.

Bezos scoffs at overly confident employees who presume they can devote a minimal amount of time to crafting such a memo. He believes getting the written word right can take a week or more to accomplish: "The great memos are written and re-written, shared with colleagues who are asked to improve the work, set aside for a couple of days, and then edited again with a fresh mind."[81]

Beyond the meeting memo, Amazon uses the written word to create clarity for most every major decision.[82] In the words of one Amazon vice president, "Almost every meeting which involves making a business decision is driven by a document.... One of the great things about a written document is that it drives a lot of clarity in the process."[83]

Amazon has had so much success in driving clarity and innovation via narrative that other companies, like JPMorgan Chase, are trying to replicate the practice.[84]

FASHIONED NOT FOUND

Strategists are zealots for the written word. If clarity is a superpower, strategists know writing is their best medium for validating it.

Don't allow any promising idea to go unwritten. Force yourself and those around you to write it down. Then rewrite it. And then rewrite your rewrite.

If your writing feels bulky, keep reading William Zinsser's *On Writing Well* to declare war on wasted words. Zinsser is direct: "Clutter is the disease of American writing....The secret of good writing is to strip every sentence to its cleanest components."[85]

The best modern-day adaptation of Zinsser's work is *Smart Brevity: The Power of Saying More with Less* by the founders of *Axios* and *Politico*.[86] Their mantra hangs on a sign in their newsroom: "Brevity is confidence. Length is fear."[87]

If your writing feels blurry, ask your colleagues to read your piece and summarize your main points back to you. If their comprehension is sharp, your work is too good not to be better. If their interpretation differs from your intention, trust you have a lot more work to do.

If your writing feels banal, don't settle for second-rate results. Your writing is a commentary on your thinking. Uninspired writing has no chance of capturing the magic of inspired thinking. Pick a few talented writers and read their work multiple times. Internalize. Imitate. Iterate. Read writers talking about writing.

Above all, keep writing.

Clarity comes from torturing your ideas until they confess their highest truth, their essence. The illustrator Christoph Niemann confirms as much: "The only path to success is through mountains of killed ideas."[88]

STRATEGIST'S NOTEBOOK

FILTER EVERYTHING

The philosopher Michel Foucault is best known for his theories on the relationship between knowledge and power. For Foucault, knowledge entails more than the mere transmission of ideas from one person to another. It is, above all, an exercise in power. Because the way one person shapes knowledge has the power to profoundly influence how another receives it.

FREE THOUGHT FROM WHAT IT THINKS

Foucault's work unearths how power shapes all aspects of knowledge—from creation to organization to dissemination. Foucault captures this nuance best when he suggests one's aim should be to "free thought from what it silently thinks, and so enable it to think differently."[89] In other words, you must be capable of stripping away the hidden assumptions and agendas within any line of thinking.

Keep Foucault's wisdom handy for a simple reason: It disciplines you to slow down and deliberately think about your thinking—to interrogate the default settings embedded in received information.

Strategists must be deliberate thinkers, not default thinkers.

Strategy work, like it or not, relies heavily on information delivered from others via presentations, reports, data sets, observations, and verbal accounts. It's terribly easy to start running with this information before assessing its quality. Why?

Time pressure is often a culprit. The strategy you are expected to build was needed yesterday, not tomorrow. Trust plays a role too. Since you trust the individual providing the information, you don't feel the need to test its accuracy.

Resist the rationalizations. Don't be rushed. Don't be handled. Don't be naive. And don't accept the default settings. Filter everything that comes your way.

Consider diamonds as a useful analogy.

Diamonds are differentiated by a careful grading of the 4 C's: cut, color, clarity, and carat weight. Buyers and sellers use this multifaceted assessment to make sense of a diamond's rarity, value, and pricing. Even unsavvy consumers know it's unwise to buy or sell a diamond without first knowing these background details.

Strategists think of received information in much the same way. They break down the information they receive into component parts and grade the value of each.

> **Cut:** Who organized this information, and what biases do they bring to the table?

> **Color:** Does anyone interpret this information differently than the consensus view?

> **Clarity:** What's missing from this rendering of reality and why?

> **Carat Weight:** Is the dependability and durability of the information getting stronger or weaker as a result of clarifying questions?

The goal is to keep filtering the information to achieve a more refined view of the reality being presented to you at this particular time.

COLIN POWELL'S FOUR-STEP RULE

General Colin Powell, a lifelong strategist in multiple domains, was smart enough to train his team to deliver information to him in a pre-filtered way. His instructions to them were crystal clear based on a simple four-step rule:

1. Tell me what you know,

2. Tell me what you don't know,

3. Tell me what you think, and

4. Always distinguish which from which.[90]

General Powell's framework hints at a potential flaw in most information gathering. It's hard to discern where the facts stop and the story starts. Think of it this way: The facts are the what and when of a situation, while the story is the why and how.

FACTS STOP AND THE STORY STARTS

Imagine a direct report tells you three employees in another manager's unit resigned last week. This type of what and when information is straightforward. It happened, or it didn't. And this fact can be easily verified.

The story kicks in as soon as the narrator ventures beyond reciting the facts and suggests why the resignations occurred (e.g., they felt micromanaged) and how this relates to a predicted outcome (e.g., if you don't want other folks to leave, it's best to remove their boss).

See how naturally a story can flow into causation, attribution, and conclusions?

Discerning where the facts stop and the story starts is critical when receiving information from any source.

And never more so than in a time of crisis, when you're required to make timely decisions with partial information. If your partial information is imprecise or overdetermined based on the storytelling involved, your chance of making the right call suffers dramatically.

THIRD EAR
In filtering information, remember to listen at a deeper level than what's being said. A key concept among psychoanalysts is to listen for what a client is *not* saying within the context of what they *are* saying. What's the unsaid insight buried beneath the said expression? Psychoanalysts call this technique listening with your third ear. Strategists must do the same.

THINK IN QUESTIONS

Strategists think in questions. They can be questions of where or how, why or when, what or what if. There's no formula to follow nor a perfect question that works every time. Only the reality that questions force you to think differently. And doing so upends the default thinking lurking within and around you.

To better understand the power of inquiry, it's hard not to begin with Warren Berger. Berger is a self-described "questionologist." Translation: he's obsessed with studying the art and science of questioning.

Berger's first book, *A More Beautiful Question*, details how several innovative companies got their breakthrough success by seeking to answer a burning question.[91] His central thesis: Inquiry is the precursor to innovation. Ask more and better questions and unlock more and better innovative ideas and insights.

The innovators at Google's moonshot factory, known as X, would agree with Berger. In tackling moonshot projects, these trailblazers start by skipping potential answers and focusing instead on finding the right questions.[92]

To thrive in today's fast-changing world, Berger believes questions are fast becoming more valuable than answers. His book *The Book of Beautiful Questions* serves as a practical guide on how to fully integrate questions into your everyday life.[93] It contains more than four hundred questions to stimulate your thinking.

If inquiry were a muscle, Berger would be your ideal trainer. It's hard to engage with his work and not find yourself thinking in questions.

BRAINSTORMING IN QUESTIONS

Another way to uncover the power of inquiry is to invert brainstorming.

Historically, brainstorming has focused on generating answers. Disenchanted with traditional brainstorming, Hal Gregersen spontaneously challenged his students at MIT's Sloan School of Management to do the opposite: brainstorm in questions.[94] This atypical exercise, recounts Gregersen, led to deeper insights, less defensiveness, better energy, and more fresh perspectives. How does it work?

Gregersen has two inflexible rules for brainstorming in questions. First, you can only contribute questions, not thinly veiled answers to another's question. Second, no preambles or explanations tied to your question. In other words, questions must be pure questions.

The duration of the exercise is critical, too. Gregersen recommends four minutes or a minimum target of fifteen questions, whichever comes first. Why the rigid structure? The time pressure helps the group maintain a singular focus on generating questions.

Gregersen also recommends devoting more than one round to a given brainstorming session. More rounds generate more uncommon perspectives, which is critical to unearthing fresh and creative ideas.

Gregersen's last piece of advice is perhaps his most pointed: don't allow the great ideas, insights, and energy that flow from this new form of brainstorming to go unused or underappreciated. Following up on the best questions sends a clear and consistent message to your team that inquiry matters to your organization.

What started as a casual, frustration-ridden suggestion to his students eventually led Gregersen to build a consulting practice devoted to brainstorming in questions, which he eventually dubbed the "Question Burst" technique. His fieldwork, coupled with findings from interviewing two hundred creative thinkers, became the theoretical backbone for the book *Questions Are the Answer*.[95]

THE POWER OF INQUIRY

Okay, you're sold on the power of inquiry. Now what? Start with three steps:

❶ *Consider inquiry to be a vocational calling.*

Consider the 80/20 rule for listening as a helpful analogy. It suggests leaders should listen for 80 percent of the time and limit speaking to 20 percent. Strategists should treat inquiry the same way: Devote 80 percent of your speaking time to asking questions and 20 percent to everything else.

Reluctant to try? Take the strategist John Hagel's observation to heart: "Leaders who ask powerful questions have the greatest success in both seizing new opportunities and addressing unexpected challenges—and they build cultures that will carry these benefits into the future."[96]

❷ *Discover what undermines the power of questioning and guard against it.*

Avoid leading questions, such as, "Don't you think my idea deserves more attention?" Such self-serving framing causes your personal agenda to drive the discussion, not the real issue at hand. Also, never weaponize your question to attack someone or something else. Finally, abstain from asking inane questions.

Ben Horowitz, author and venture capitalist, has a notable strategy for dealing with hollow questions:

He doesn't answer them.[97] According to Horowitz, many of the CEOs he works with will ask for his advice in the form of a question. That's their prepared question, explains Horowitz, and what they are really asking for is his approval of their preconceived answer. Instead of answering, Horowitz responds with his own series of questions that seeks to unearth the deeper issues at play.

❸ *Treat questioning as a craft that must be practiced and perfected.*

The key is to get the framing right. Gregersen believes the most productive questions are "open versus closed, short versus long, and simple versus complex."[98]

One way to keep Gregersen's advice top of mind is to routinely ask: What's the smartest dumb question to ask here? This mental reminder keeps your questions simple, clear, and crisp.

A well-framed question represents your best chance of unlocking the idea, insight, or follow-up question that can move your team's thinking to the next level. The business writer Leigh Buchanan says it best: "The right questions don't allow people to remain passive. They require reflection, followed by action."[99]

In taking Buchanan's insight a step further, never fail to ask a more profound question of your question: Is this question I am about to share dead or alive?

Dead questions sink.
Live questions swim.
Profound questions sail.

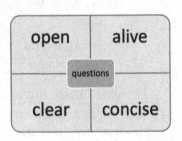

BUILDING UP YOUR QUESTION BANK

Keep a running list of useful questions at the ready. Map them to particular situations such as driving clarity, advancing coaching, disrupting defaults, or leading change.

Here are ten deposits to your question bank:

1. If you had to boil down this discussion to a question, what would it be for you?

2. Is there a deeper question buried beneath the current one for you?

3. If you had more time, how would you approach this decision differently?

4. Where is clarity lacking, and how can you get it?

5. What matters most in this discussion for you?

6. If this organization disappeared today, what would be different tomorrow?[100]

7. What will be the implication ten minutes, ten months, and ten years from now?

8. If a colleague were making this decision, what advice would you give them?

9. What is *not* going to change in the next ten years?[101]

10. What would it take for the group to change their minds?[102]

This last question comes from Google's chief decision scientist, Cassie Kozyrkov. In Kozyrkov's words, "Most people don't ask this question enough and you might be surprised how much your team's decision-making improves when you start every decision with it."[103]

Kozyrkov continues, "Coming up with an answer forces the team to confront their pre-existing opinions, identify the extent to which their mind is already set, understand how they navigate their context, clarify their assumptions, declare the information they need, and add structure to the decision process. It also adds a layer of protection against cognitive biases like confirmation bias."[104]

Strategists know questions are the midwife of strategy. If your strategy isn't born and raised on sound questions, ones that are well crafted and wisely refined, be prepared to live with the uninspired results that come from thinking in answers.

If you choose to anchor your strategy in inquiry, remember Colum McCann's advice: "Keep yourself away from answers, but alive in the middle of the question."[105]

STRATEGIST'S NOTEBOOK

WHY NOT?

Simon Sinek believes great leaders have at least one thing in common—they start with the question of why.[106] That's because they realize individuals won't fully invest in an idea, vision, movement, or product until they understand the why behind it.

If great leaders know the power of explaining the why, great strategists know one better—the hidden advantage of exploring the why not.

In *Farsighted: How We Make the Decisions That Matter the Most,* Steven Johnson provides a fascinating account of the complex strategy work that led to the capture and killing of Osama bin Laden.[107] It's a poignant case study of the power of asking why not.

THE HUNT FOR OSAMA BIN LADEN

Following the terrorist attacks on September 11, 2001, the US intelligence community devoted nearly a decade to determining the whereabouts of Osama bin Laden. By November 2010, some intelligence analysts had a working theory that bin Laden was hiding in a residential compound in Abbottabad, Pakistan. Their certainty level? It varied from 60 to 90 percent. Their problem? They had no hard evidence to confirm their assessment.

One of the senior officials the analysts needed to convince was John Brennan, Obama's counterterrorism adviser at the time. A career intelligence professional, Brennan was well aware of the subtle role cognitive biases play in shaping intelligence assessments. At one point in the process, Brennan told the analysts, "I'm tired of hearing why everything you see confirms your case.... What we need to look for are the things that tell us what's not right about our theory."[108]

Brennan effectively challenged the analysts to utilize the mental construct of "why not" to stress-test their conclusion regarding bin Laden's whereabouts. In other words, why is the mysterious man in the compound not the most wanted person in the world?

WHY NOT

When the analysts came back to the White House to present their theories of why not, per Brennan's direction, something fascinating happened. One of their theories as to why it couldn't be Osama bin Laden hiding in the high-walled compound involved a satellite image of a dog on the premises. Their conventional thinking was that no devout, self-respecting Muslim leader of bin Laden's stature would have a dog with him.

It was only then that Brennan had a breakthrough insight. He recalled bin Laden, unbeknownst to many in the intelligence community, had lived with dogs during his time in Sudan in the mid-1990s.

This "why not" exercise with Brennan, which unlocked the meaning behind a pivotal piece of existing intelligence, provided the Obama administration with the degree of confidence they needed to move forward with planning the raid on the Abbottabad compound.

Nevertheless, even after Brennan's breakthrough insight about bin Laden's connection to dogs, the Obama administration continued its due diligence by pursuing two parallel paths.

On the one hand, Admiral William McRaven led SEAL Team Six through a series of training raids on a simulated compound located on military bases in North Carolina and Nevada. On the other hand, the Obama administration charged a "red team" with conducting yet another "why not" exercise regarding bin Laden's whereabouts.

RED TEAM

In the military, a red team plays the formal role of devil's advocate.[109]

The team is designed to be independent, having had no role in crafting the information at hand. The team is also expected to be relentless in rethinking every aspect of the argument—questioning assumptions, deconstructing evidence, generating alternative explanations, assigning predictability rates to certain conclusions, and so on.

In short, a red team functions like a "why not" think tank.

After questioning the theory that bin Laden was hiding in a residential compound in Abbottabad, Obama's red team adjusted their certainty level down to less than 50 percent.[110] Even so, the Obama administration was comfortable enough with their due diligence to proceed with their clandestine mission. On May 2, 2011, SEAL Team Six raided the high-walled compound under the cover of darkness and captured and killed Osama bin Laden.

LESSONS LEARNED

As a strategist, what lessons can you learn from this behind-the-scenes account of the capture and killing of Osama bin Laden?

① *Developing a sound strategy takes time and unhurried due diligence.*
Consider the timeline above. Though the Obama administration had a lead on bin Laden's whereabouts as early as November 2010, they didn't launch the official mission until May 2011.

Think of the discipline it took to wait six months to solidify their strategy and overprepare for their mission. Recall that bin Laden was the most wanted person in the world at the time. Every day they didn't act to capture or kill him only increased the risk of bin Laden secretly moving to another location.

And yet, as Johnson reports, McRaven spent months practicing on the simulated raids—so much so that he "had a backup for every possible failure, and a backup to the failure of the backup, and a backup to the failure of the backup of the backup."[111]

② *Determine in advance what level of confidence you will need to greenlight the launch of your strategy.*

In the case of the bin Laden raid, it's worth underscoring the mission's biggest risk. Though SEAL Team Six had trained for every possible scenario, they stormed the compound still not knowing if bin Laden was actually there. Despite a lack of hard evidence to anchor their decision, the Obama administration had achieved the confidence level they needed in their strategy work to move forward with the historic mission.

③ *Put something meaningful on the line when pursuing your strategy.*
Low stakes tend to produce uninspiring results. High stakes, meanwhile, often bring out the best performances, leading to bold results.

For the Obama administration, conducting a military raid in Pakistan without that government's knowledge was rife with risk and consequence. If American lives had been lost, many would have second-guessed the decision to pursue a complex air-to-ground invasion rather than deploying a drone strike. If Pakistani lives had been lost, the geopolitics of the region would have been destabilized.

With the stakes so high, the Obama administration's strategy had real lives—not to mention their reputation—hanging in the balance.

④ *When building your strategy, carve out time to conduct the "why not" exercise.*

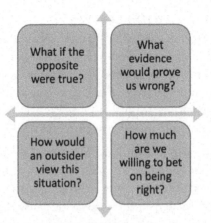

Better still, take a page from the military's play-book and establish a red team to do it for you. Having a formal team to perform the role of devil's advocate is far more effective than simply doing it yourself on the fly. As Johnson explains, "red teams force you to take on a new perspective, or consider an alternate narrative, that might not easily come to mind in a few minutes of casual devil's advocacy."[112]

Netflix has a standard practice of "farming for dissent" when building a strategy.[113] Employees are strongly encouraged to seek critical feedback from others on what might be wrong, missing, or unclear about their ideas and assumptions.

As Netflix's founder Reed Hastings explains, "We now say that it is disloyal to Netflix when you disagree with an idea and do **not** express that disagreement. By withholding your opinion, you are implicitly choosing to not help the company."[114]

RUN A GOOD PROCESS

As recently as 2020, Barack Obama reflected on this historic decision-making process involving bin Laden and concluded, "It was an operation rife with uncertainty and risk. So, I ran a tight process. I trusted my team. I listened to every voice in the room. I gave myself space to think."[115]

Strategists always look for ways to guard against default thinking. They know stress-testing ideas is a must. That certainty is a mirage. That quick and universal agreement is cause for pause. That running ideas frontwards and backwards—exploring the why and, importantly, the why not—is essential. That hunches need time to breathe. That guarantees are a fool's game.

And, lastly, strategists keep the words of J. K. Galbraith top of mind: "Faced with the choice between changing one's mind and proving that there is no need to do so, almost everyone gets busy on the proof."[116]

Everyone but the strategist.

PUSH UPSTREAM

What new product should you create? What emerging market can you help define? How can you become the premier innovator in your industry?

Such big-picture strategy work can be exhilarating. But it can't be the only page in your strategy playbook. Strategists must also be able to solve tough problems in the here and now.

Problems are easy to neglect. Why? Because the rationalizations for looking the other way tend to stick. For instance, it's often assumed that fixing the problem will take too long. Or will cost too much. Or will cause unwanted drama. Or will undermine other priorities. Another common refrain is the blame game: "We didn't break it, so why do we have to fix it?"

Such alibis have an impressive record of prompting leaders to kick the can down the road.

Save for General Colin Powell. He lived by a simple creed: "Never walk past a mistake."[117]

Powell's theory is grounded in the law of accumulation. If you allow mistakes to stand, even minor ones, you create an environment for them to safely multiply, and ultimately magnify, into a major breakdown.[118] Strategists know mistakes, like problems, must be attacked rather than ignored—or else, they multiply and mutate.

STRATEGY: PROBLEM SPOTTING AND SOLVING

The strategist Richard Rumelt doubles down on this logic.[119] He believes in a challenge-based approach to strategy—one that focuses on confronting problems, not chasing platitudes. He implores strategists to always, without fail, start by diagnosing the crux of the problem.

Rumelt follows a three-step process for spotting problems: 1) Collect: develop a list of all challenges and issues; 2) Cluster: organize them into compatible groups; and 3) Filter: determine those that are critical and solvable.[120]

Only after the crux of a problem has been identified and analyzed should attention shift, in Rumelt's view, to generating options and prioritizing action steps.

As Rumelt explains, "To have someone believe in you and trust in your strategy, there has to be a logic and argument, and some evidence, as to how you are dealing with the challenges you face."[121]

DOWNSTREAM

For Dan Heath, problem-solving is more a matter of where than how. In *Upstream: The Quest to Solve Problems Before They Happen*, Heath claims most problems get managed too far downstream.[122]

Downstream problems invariably flirt with disaster. Hence the language of fire extinguished, day saved, or crisis averted. These problems often get patched right before a meltdown ensues. Since last-second heroics tend to be highly visible and satisfying, most societies celebrate the rescue or recovery.[123]

Yet doing so only reinforces the habit of reacting, of staying downstream. And if you spend so much of your thinking and doing reacting to problems, you seem less inclined to ask if these challenges could be prevented in the first place.[124]

Downstream is the land of symptoms. Imagine an endless game of whack-a-mole, whereby you spend a ton of time, energy, and resources beating down different surges of the same problem. Yes, it may feel like you're winning that day, given how much effort you've expended. But the truth is inescapable: You're playing the wrong game.

Heath recounts a story from the travel company Expedia to illustrate the costs associated with downstream behavior.[125] In 2012, two executives discovered a major anomaly in the data related to Expedia's call center. For every one hundred customers who booked travel on the website, fifty-eight of them called soon after for help.[126]

In mining the data, the executives realized twenty million of these annual calls resulted from a single issue: Since customers lacked an easy way to retrieve their travel itinerary from the website after a booking, they contacted the call center to get it. At the time, Expedia spent roughly five dollars per call to keep the call center staffed and supported. Therefore, this one previously overlooked problem was costing the company $100 million annually.

What did Expedia's CEO do with this information? He traveled upstream. He pulled together a team from different parts of the company and gave them a clear-cut, upstream objective: "Save customers from needing to call us."[127]

The strategy worked. Rather than simply fixing the immediate problem, the team developed a multipronged solution that fixed several other friction points for customers as well. As a result, calls to Expedia's call center declined from 58 percent to 15 percent, saving the company several millions of dollars annually in the process.

UPSTREAM

Strategists work upstream rather than downstream.

They focus on sources, not symptoms. They want to fix a problem for good. Better still, they want to prevent it from happening in the first place.

To push upstream, strategists concentrate on the four Ps: principled, practical, perceptive, and persistent.

❶ *Strategists are principled.*

They refuse to allow a problem to be defined as natural or inevitable.[128] If a problem can be created, they believe it can be uncreated. They are allergic to excuses and addicted to results.

❷ *Strategists are practical.*

They believe problems must be owned before they can be solved.[129] That's why they have zero interest in prosecuting the past via the blame game. They would rather spend their time and resources on bending the future in their desired direction.

❸ *Strategists are perceptive.*

They know a one-off solution to a problem is rarely enough. What's needed are upstream systems that are smart, systematic, and sustainable, ones that detect problems early, bring the best ideas to the fore, solve the problem in totality, and reproduce success time after time.

Take customer fulfillment as an example. Amazon ships more than one million packages a day. How many get missorted on their watch? Fewer than four.[130] Yes, read that again—fewer than four in a million. Solutions compete. Systems win.

❹ *Strategists are persistent.*

They don't give up or give in. They are relentless in their drive to push upstream. Strategists, in the words of Cormac McCarthy, work hard to "keep a little fire burning: however small, however hidden."[131]

THE DIFFERENCE

Moving your strategy work upstream can be a heavy lift, especially early on.

Working upstream requires better forecasting, data, analysis, debate, coordination, systems thinking, and long-term investment. All of this can come with a hefty price tag. But take a moment to recognize the more troubling costs associated with living downstream.

Lastly, learning how to work upstream effectively and efficiently takes practice and patience for everyone involved. If you fail to experiment with working upstream in good times, how can you reasonably expect your organization to get there in bad times?

Strategists know the best way to guard against downstream thinking is to move themselves and their organization upstream as soon as possible.

DOWNSTREAM	vs.	UPSTREAM
symptoms	→	sources
blame	→	own
urgent	→	essential
shortsighted	→	farsighted
parts	→	whole
patch	→	solve

STRATEGIST'S NOTEBOOK

KILL FRICTION

For some strategists, the biggest challenge is knowing where to start. If you struggle to defeat the blank page, focus on a single strategic aim: kill friction.

Friction represents the speedbumps, detours, or road-blocks that keep things from running smoothly for your organization. Friction can keep your internal processes from being effective. And friction can keep your customers from feeling satisfied. Though examples of friction differ, the net result is the same: friction steals time. And losing time—yours or your customers'—is a remarkably bad strategy.

Friction leads to frustration, fatigue, and, eventually, flight.

FROM IMPORTANT TO ESSENTIAL

Christiane Lemieux, author of *Frictionless: Why the Future of Everything Will Be Fast, Fluid, and Made Just for You,* believes the best organizations declare war on friction.[132] In an increasingly digital world, these forward-looking organizations realize that current and potential customers demand nothing less.

Digital-savvy consumers, who have no patience for friction-filled experiences, will vote with their feet by leaving your product or service behind. And if you aren't actively working to kill friction, bet a competitor is seeking to exploit this strategic mistake for their gain.[133]

AMAZON'S WAR ON FRICTION

Few organizations have done more to declare war on friction than Amazon.

John Rossman considers Amazon's war on friction to be their most successful strategy of all time.[134] He ranks Amazon's frictionless solutions—such as Free Everyday Shipping, Prime Loyalty, and Item Authority—as more innovative and impactful than high-tech products such as drones, cloud computing, and Alexa.[135] Why?

Because removing the friction from shopping, selling, and shipping has redefined the nature of competition and consumerism the world over.[136] If killing friction has been the secret to Amazon's runaway success, what's holding back your organization from doing the same?

HOW TO START

How do you start building a strategy to remove or reduce friction? Rossman suggests two exercises.

First, presume you are a new customer who is engaging with the product or service for the first time.[137] Deconstruct every step of a new customer's journey with your product or service.

Are all steps associated with your product or service—buying, using, fixing, or returning—truly necessary? Which steps take too much time? Which steps are confusing? Which steps could be combined? What makes the helpful steps so effective? What's not intuitive about this process?

In probing such questions, your aim is to unearth the pressure points in your customers' experience and determine why your organization has been unable or unwilling to address them.

Second, imagine you are having a terrible customer experience with the product or service.[138] Envision how a customer's experience with your product or service might go wrong.

SIGNS OF FRICTION	
slow	taxing
complicated	hoops
confusing	layers

Why did your customer give up on navigating your website? Why did it take them so long to figure out the basic features of your product or service?

Why did they find it necessary to ask to speak with a supervisor when they called for help? How long did it take for them to get their issue resolved?

Did their experience with your customer support make them more or less likely to recommend you to a friend?

Here your aim is to anticipate the worst friction points your customer could encounter and then build a strategy to eliminate them before they arise.

No doubt Amazon had this anticipation mindset at play when they designed the Kindle Fire.[139] Any customer who experiences technical difficulties with the Kindle Fire can simply push the "Mayday" button to connect with an Amazon customer service agent who can—with the customer's permission—gain access to their device and fix the problem remotely.[140]

No anxiety about understanding the agent's technical jargon. No driving to a store and waiting in line for help. No hassle of shipping the device to a service center for repair. In other words, no friction in getting customers back to using the device effectively.

Sure, when it comes to fighting friction, Amazon is both a paragon and a pacesetter. But a growing number of successful companies have turned the corner in removing or reducing friction.

Who took friction out of finding information? Google and Wikipedia.

Who took friction out of managing life on the go? Apple.

Who took friction out of finding music? Spotify and Pandora.

Who took friction out of watching movies anywhere? Netflix.

Who took friction out of securing transportation? Uber and Lyft.

Who took friction out of securing lodging? Airbnb and VRBO.

Who took friction out of booking travel plans? Expedia and Priceline.

Who took friction out of buying insurance? GEICO.

Who took friction out of working remotely? Slack and Zoom.

FRICTION REMAINS

Though some organizations are winning the battles, be assured friction is not losing the war. Just look at the breadth and depth of friction in government, hospitals, pharmacies, education, policing, politics, real estate, law, banking, farming, and voting.

And don't be surprised when consumers start spotlighting your friction in unflattering ways. Doubtful? Just ask McDonald's if they remember the name Rashiq Zahid.[141]

Fed up with McDonald's ice cream machines constantly being broken, this frustrated customer, who happens to be a software engineer by training, managed to reverse-engineer McDonald's own app to show which stores across America currently have nonworking ice cream machines.

Zahid then created a website, aptly named mcbroken.com, to track the information in real

time, helping other customers avoid the friction of finding out the ice cream machine is broken only after they have already arrived at the store.

What's your organization's equivalent of McDonald's ice cream machines?

FRICTIONLESS: FOCUS ON THE WHO
Killing friction is a winning strategy in today's world.

But notice the extent to which striving for a frictionless environment tends to focus on a how or what, with the how being a process, such as buying, selling, or shipping, and the what being the experience of a product or service.

What if your organization also extended this focus on being frictionless to a who?

What if your organization declared war on the friction that keeps leaders and followers from becoming strategists? On the flip side, what if your organization increased the friction associated with being a non-strategist, making it harder for them to think and act in nonstrategic ways?

SEE AROUND CORNERS

The gun debuted more than a millennium ago. Soon thereafter, a simple reality hardened into an unassailable truth: Guns can't shoot around corners. Everyone accepted this truth for centuries; everyone save for Amos Golan.

In 2003, Golan invented CornerShot for SWAT teams and special forces units. CornerShot is a hinged mechanism that positions a pistol, camera, and flashlight around a corner. Meanwhile, the trigger and a camera screen remain behind the bend, allowing the shooter to safely see, aim and shoot around the corner without physically being in harm's way.

Strategists must champion the same iconoclastic belief that propelled Golan to pursue his game-changing invention. Seeing around corners is difficult, but by no means impossible, to do. You simply need a sound system to ground and guide your efforts.

For strategists, this framework is forecasting.

FORECASTING

Forecasting is a prediction of the probability of how the future may unfold. Many people steer clear of predictions because the odds of being right are rarely in their favor.

Perhaps they remember Warren Buffett's offer to pay $1 billion to anyone who picked a perfect bracket for the 2014 NCAA men's basketball tournament. The Oracle of Omaha never paid a winner because nobody has ever predicted a perfect bracket in the history of March Madness (the odds are roughly 1 in 2.4 trillion).[142]

Other people aren't so reluctant or modest when it comes to forecasting. Talking heads make their rounds in the media, predicting the future of everything from politics, stock markets, and technology to wars, salvation, and sports.

To be clear: Everyone is a forecaster.

You predict one driving route to work will be faster than another. You predict your partner will love this birthday present more than that one. You predict you will forget to complete a task later in the day, so you write yourself a reminder. Such mundane predictions happen every day, and most people make them with little thought or preparation.

Other forecasts are more complex and consequential, such as getting married, buying a house, or launching a business. Will this bet be successful? Given the stakes involved, most people devote considerable time and energy to these life-altering predictions.

Though forecasting is common, the practice of analyzing the accuracy of predictions after the fact is quite rare. The same goes for the talking heads—they prefer to sell their future predictions rather than discuss the accuracy of their past predictions.

Philip Tetlock has devoted much of his career to studying forecasting. In the 1980s, he gathered a cadre of recognized experts in various fields and asked them to make thousands of predictions about the future. Twenty years later, he evaluated these predictions and concluded the average expert was basically as accurate as "a dart-throwing chimpanzee."[143]

Tetlock's *Expert Political Judgment: How Good Is It? How Can We Know?* got plenty of people talking about the relationship between prediction and accuracy.[144] It also got Tetlock thinking more about the next phase of his forecasting research—namely, whether nonexperts could actually outperform experts (and dart-throwing chimps) in forecasting the future if provided a level playing field.

In 2011, Tetlock and his research colleagues started The Good Judgment Project (GJP), a forum for volunteers from all walks of life to try their hand at predicting global events.[145] Soon the GJP was invited to field a team in a forecasting tournament sponsored by the Intelligence Advanced Research Projects Activity (IARPA), an agency within the US intelligence community that funds research on forecasting.

The tournament included four other forecasting teams, including an independent control group, and each had to submit daily predictions at the same time for four years. To make comparative assessments easier, each team had to offer predictions on the same questions—the kind of queries professional intelligence analysts grapple with every day.

In year one, IARPA wanted the other four teams to beat the control group by 20 percent. By year four, IARPA hoped the margin of victory would grow as high as 50 percent. How did the GJP fare against these high expectations?

The GJP, a team of volunteers from various walks of life with no formal training in analyzing geopolitical intelligence, beat the control group by 60 percent in year one, and then by 78 percent in year two.

SUPERFORECASTERS

Why was the GJP so dominant?

In *Superforecasting: The Art and Science of Prediction*, Tetlock recounts the story of the GJP. He shares his findings on what distinguishes a good forecaster from a bad one—as well as a good one from a great one, a superforecaster.

Tetlock believes superforecasters share a common set of habits.

Superforecasters triage their time. They don't pursue easy questions or impenetrable ones because neither is particularly effective or efficient in helping them hone their craft. Rather, superforecasters pursue challenging but predictable questions that allow them to maximize their focus, gauge their accuracy, and identify areas for continuous improvement.

Superforecasters break big questions into smaller ones. This unpacking enables them to parse knowable from unknowable parts, assigning weighted values to each. From the outset, they attempt to establish an outside point of view by asking: "How often do things of this sort happen in situations of this sort?"[146] They use this knowable data point as an anchor to calibrate their initial thinking before exploring more inside questions of uniqueness and specificity.

Superforecasters update their beliefs routinely and meticulously. Tetlock's research found the strongest predictor of what made a good forecaster become a superforecaster was the individual's level of commitment to belief updating and self-improvement. "For superforecasters, beliefs are hypothesis to be tested, not treasures to be guarded."[147]

In other words, superforecasters first form a provisional forecast. Then, they spend the remainder of their allotted time gathering new information, testing assumptions, sharpening granular judgments, and refining conclusions. In the process, they learn to guard against cognitive biases, such as overestimating or underestimating evidence, refusing to believe the opposite could be true, and conflating facts with values.

Superforecasters insist on learning from their results, both the wins and especially the losses. They study the quality of thinking behind their decisions. What evidence worked best? What assumptions proved most flawed? Where did luck factor into the equation?

Lastly, **superforecasters tend to see distinct value in working with others to stress-test their ideas and assumptions.** And the results reveal the same. Tetlock's research shows teams were 23 percent more accurate than individual forecasters on average.[148]

LESSON LEARNED

You can't be a good strategist and a bad forecaster at the same time.

If strategy's purpose is to bridge the gulf between here and now and there and then, every strategist must be a skilled forecaster. Better still, strive to be a superforecaster. Because you can't reasonably expect to shape the future, much less win it, if you're unable to anticipate its contours.

A telling example to remember is John Antioco.[149] In 2000, Antioco led a company worth $6 billion that controlled roughly one-third of the video rental market. He then raised $465 million to capture even more market share. At the time, two cofounders of a fledgling DVD start-up company met with Antioco and offered to sell him their business for $50 million. Antioco promptly declined and sent them on their way.

Fast-forward ten years: the company Antioco had led files for bankruptcy. At the time, Blockbuster was valued at less than $25 million. Meanwhile, the two cofounders, Reed Hastings and Marc Randolph, had built their DVD company into a $13 billion business by 2010. And today, Netflix is valued north of $250 billion.

The lesson learned? Antioco isn't the first person to make the wrong bet on a lottery winner. Ronald Wayne, as the legendary story goes, sold his 10 percent stake in Apple for $800 back in 1976. (Yes, you read that right.) The reason to remember Antioco's time at Blockbuster is that he failed to think and act like a capable forecaster.

In the meeting with Hastings and Randolph, Antioco reportedly said: "The dot-com hysteria is completely overblown."[150] True, circa 2000, Antioco wasn't the only business leader skeptical of online business models. But how long did it take him to update and edit his beliefs on the fast-evolving nature of online behavior and consumption?

Antioco waited until 2004, six years after Netflix's arrival on the scene, to launch a new DVD subscription service called Blockbuster Online. By this time, Netflix had already secured the high ground in the DVD subscription space with more than $500 million in revenue.

Perhaps the most obvious sign of Antioco's shortsightedness is that he never made Hastings and Randolph an offer or counteroffer to buy Netflix. That's a revealing contrast to Jeff Bezos, who reportedly offered Hastings and Randolph low eight figures to buy Netflix in 1998—when the company was only two months old.

SEE AROUND CORNERS

Strategists have much to learn from superforecasters. As you seek to improve your forecasting skills, keep these seven goals top of mind:

1) Pick your playing field wisely.

2) Break big unknown questions into smaller known parts; assign probabilities.

3) Take the outside view before exploring inside angles.

4) Treat your beliefs as under construction; update them early and often.

5) Guard against cognitive biases.

6) Practice your craft; keep score; always be learning.

7) Never tire of trying, failing, analyzing, adjusting, and trying again.[151]

Strategists know their work is aimless unless it's moored to a well-crafted, continuously revised theory of things to come. That's the only way to see around corners.

The strategist Ram Charan believes seeing around corners—spotting anomalies, sensing trends, and detecting warning signs—is a teachable skill that increasingly defines successful leadership in the modern era.[152] Charan calls it the attacker's advantage: "...the ability to detect ahead of others those forces that are radically reshaping your marketplace, then position your business to make the next move first."[153]

How do you get started in building your forecasting skills?

Start small to grow big. Keep a log of your forecasts. What are you seeing before others? In scoring your predictions, what did you get wrong and why?

Keep a list of attackers. What did they see in the external landscape before others? How did they navigate their own biases? How did they position their organization to take advantage of the situation and go on the offensive?

STRATEGIST'S NOTEBOOK

FIVE FORCES

Michael Porter is considered the primary architect of modern business strategy. With 20 books and 130 articles to his name, even his critics can't deny Porter's widespread success and longstanding appeal.

Porter's 1979 article, "How Competitive Forces Shape Strategy," was deemed a must-read in management circles.[154] The next year, he published *Competitive Strategy*, which ranks among the most influential management books of the twentieth century.[155] And his 1996 article "What Is Strategy?" is one of the most-cited, bestselling reads from *Harvard Business Review*.[156]

Every strategist should have a working knowledge of Porter's work. Not because his theories are the gospel. But because the shadow of his influence is so long.

Porter's former student and longtime collaborator, Joan Magretta, has synthesized his oeuvre into a single guide entitled *Understanding Michael Porter*.[157] It's the easiest path for engaging with the breadth and depth of his work.

DEFINING STRATEGY

Porter defines strategy as "how an organization, faced with competition, will achieve superior performance."[158] Competition lies at the heart of strategy for Porter. He believes those who define competition as "seeking to be the best" have already lost the strategy race because being the best is a mirage.

If a company were truly the best, it would have no competition. And for Porter, no business enjoys an environment free and clear from competition.

Instead of trying to be the best, Porter believes companies should focus on being unique. Your strategy should center on creating value and meeting customer needs in unique ways. Being unique also requires you to refrain from trying to capture or please every customer. In Porter's words, "The sign of a good strategy is that it deliberately makes some customers unhappy."[159]

Porter was the first to popularize the now-common depiction of strategy as choices, strategy as trade-offs, and strategy as deciding what *not* to do.

Porter is best known for his five forces theory. It's an analytic framework used to formulate a new strategy or evaluate an existing one. The tool is designed to deconstruct the competitive contours of your industry—everything from structural elements to value creation to profitability.

FIVE FORCES

Porter believes the following five forces shape every strategy.

1 **Bargaining power of buyers:** The aim is to determine the relative power of customers within your industry. Are they powerful enough to drive down prices or demand you deliver more value? If so, your industry's profitability will be lower, on average, as more value shifts to the buyer.

Most individual buyers lack the hefty bargaining power necessary to tip the value scale in their direction. But think of institutional buyers such as Walmart or Home Depot. Given their visibility and capacity, they have significant leverage to negotiate better terms or pricing.

2. **Bargaining power of suppliers:** If your industry includes powerful suppliers, they will be more likely to charge higher prices or negotiate better terms. More value to them means less profit to you.

Consider the power a company like Intel has in supplying preferred parts to the companies that make personal computers. Porter also includes labor unions in this category insofar as they supply companies with labor.

3. **Threat of substitute products or services:** Is your industry susceptible to having substitutes enter the market and capture customer choice? H&R Block is a prime example. Rather than being disrupted by a direct rival with a physical presence, H&R Block had to adjust to do-it-yourself software solutions such as TurboTax.

Since substitutes can emerge quickly and from unexpected places, they can be difficult to anticipate or outmaneuver. An industry that's ripe for substitutions has more of its profitability at risk.

④ **Threat of new entrants:** Is it difficult for new-comers to enter your industry and gain market share? If not, your profitability will likely suffer.

For instance, since the barrier to opening a restaurant is relatively low, the threat of new entrants is high. By contrast, it would cost nearly a billion dollars for a company to develop a new operating system for personal computers. A similarly high wall exists for entry into other research-heavy industries, such as prescription drugs, or into highly regulated areas, such as nuclear energy.

⑤ **Rivalry among existing competitors:** If an industry is defined by intense rivalry, profitability will be lower for two reasons: 1) Companies will likely offer lower prices to retain existing customers or to capture new ones, and 2) Companies will likely spend more money in head-to-head competition via marketing, advertising, new products, and so on.

If customers can easily and cheaply switch from one competitor to the next, the downside of rivalry will deepen. Additionally, if you're trying to serve the same customers in more or less the same way as your rivals, your efforts will tilt more to imitation than innovation. And it's nearly impossible to achieve superior performance, in Porter's view, by simply reacting to your competitors.

Porter's five forces speak to what he considers a universal truth: "There are a limited number of structural forces at work in every industry that *systematically* impact *profitability* in a *predictable direction.*"[160] The key is to realize your profits can be affected by multiple players in various ways, not just by a direct rival via head-to-head competition.

Strategy decisions on where to play and how to win should therefore be rooted in choices and trade-offs that flow from your five forces analysis. In other words, it's not enough merely to do the analysis: the data and insights must be leveraged to advance your competitive edge.

Finally, Porter warns against thinking your five forces analysis can stand the test of time. The realities revealed by the five forces framework are dynamic, not static. Industry economics can change dramatically and quickly.

Porter believes strategy tools are designed to live on the desk, not the shelf.

4 SKILLS

Decide Better
Message Better
Innovate Better
Coach Better

DECIDE BETTER

Since every strategy is built on a series of decisions, every strategist must be a student of decision-making. The field of decision science is growing in size and stature.

In academia, the study of decision-making spans multiple disciplines—from neuroscience, psychology, economics, and statistics to data science, computer science, and the humanities.

In business, Google established the role of chief decision scientist a few years back with the goal of systematically upgrading the quality of decision-making across the enterprise.

Still another sign decision science has arrived is the sheer number of books and articles recently published on the ins and outs of decision-making.

As a strategist, you won't regret learning as much as you can about the art and science of decision-making. Improving the quality of your decisions tends to improve the quality of your strategies and the odds of their success.

To deepen your understanding of decision-making, adapt these four strategies to your particular context:

1) Process vs. Outcome

2) The 70 Percent Rule

3) The OODA Loop

4) One-Way Doors vs. Two-Way Doors

PROCESS VS. OUTCOME

Most people judge the quality of a decision by its outcome.

If the result is favorable, they assume the process for making the decision was good. If the result is unfavorable, they deem it bad luck. In both cases, they stop short of assessing the decision process that led to the decision outcome. This is the definition of outcome bias.

Google's chief decision scientist, Cassie Kozyrkov, spends her days contemplating the architecture of decision-making—the good, the bad, and the ugly. Her advice is unequivocal: it's uncommon but essential to parse your decision process from your decision outcome if you want to effectively evaluate the quality of each component.[161]

Annie Duke, a retired poker champion turned strategy consultant, further explains this distinction between process and outcome in *Thinking in Bets: Making Smarter Decisions When You Don't Have All the Facts*.[162] As Duke details, by off-loading decision losses to bad luck and by onboarding decision wins to skill, most decision-makers never face the hard truths regarding their own biases.[163] In turn, they never learn how to improve their decision-making abilities.[164]

If there's any doubt about the power of this self-serving bias, watch these same individuals ascribe the opposite dynamic to other decision-makers. If others make a good decision, it's presumed to be the result of luck. If others make a bad decision, it's presumed to be the result of subpar decision-making skills.

The strategist Adam Grant agrees with the need to decouple the decision process from the decision outcome. He developed a straightforward framework for doing so.[165]

As Grant explains, it's shortsighted to judge the quality of your decision based solely on its outcome. If a positive outcome derives from a shallow process, it's more likely the result of luck than skill. If you keep anchoring future decisions in a shallow process, expect the outcomes to suffer as luck eventually wanes.

		DECISION OUTCOME	
		POSITIVE	NEGATIVE
DECISION PROCESS	SHALLOW	LUCK	FAILURE
	DEEP	IMPROVEMENT	EXPERIMENT

Similarly, if a deep process leads to a negative outcome, consider it a helpful experiment to gather lessons learned. For instance, identify the external conditions that shaped the unfavorable result and try to experiment with mitigating them in future decisions. The best place to land in decision-making is in the southwest quadrant of Grant's grid—crafting a deep decision process that leads to a positive outcome.

The upshot: The best decision-makers focus more on the process than on the outcome, realizing they are better positioned to shape the former than the latter. And if they improve their decision process significantly and continuously, good things tend to follow. Again, it's about improving the odds of success, not guaranteeing them.[166]

As a strategist, don't allow the outcome of a decision, especially favorable ones, to keep you from rigorously assessing the quality of your decision-making process.

A telling example of outcome bias comes from the world of professional basketball. Three economists studied 23,275 NBA games over twenty seasons and found a revealing decision pattern among coaches.[167] In close games, the difference between winning or losing can be negligible—a lucky bounce here, a bad officiating call there, or the other team makes more free throws than expected. Such developments are largely beyond the control of the players.

Yet these NBA coaches were much more likely to change their strategy—in this case, their starting lineup—for the next game if the previous one ended with a loss, albeit a narrow one. They allowed a previous decision outcome (win/loss), not the quality of a previous decision process (how the team played), to determine the structure and strategy behind their next decision.

As the researchers observed, these professional coaches, who had ascended to the top of their field, had a propensity to "switch strategies excessively after losses and not enough after wins."[168]

THE 70 PERCENT RULE

The sweeping preference in decision-making is to have more information and time than less. But what happens if a situation or competitor forces your hand, and you must decide quickly? You've analyzed some pieces of the puzzle but not all. How do you proceed?

The paragon of long-term thinking, Jeff Bezos, is known for not rushing decisions. But even Bezos knows waiting for the full spectrum of inputs to be assembled and analyzed before deciding, while appealing in theory, is problematic in practice. Because being too slow to market can be worse than breaking into the market with a not-yet-perfect product or service.

How does Bezos guard against analysis paralysis on his way to making high-stakes decisions? The 70 percent rule.

Bezos preaches the need for Amazon employees to make high-quality, high-velocity decisions.[169] One without the other, in his view, is myopic.[170] To deliver speedy decisions,

Bezos practices the 70 percent rule. Once he has studied 70 percent of the information needed to act, he moves forward in making a decision.

"If you wait for 90%, in most cases, you're probably being slow," observes Bezos.[171]

As a strategist, you must train yourself and your team to make not only high-quality but also high-velocity decisions.

OODA LOOP

The military strategist and fighter pilot John Boyd developed an agile decision-making cycle known as the OODA loop.[172] The loop includes four stages: observe, orient, decide, and act.

If teams can make better and faster decisions than their opponents, argues Boyd, they create a distinct advantage in their field of play. Originally envisioned for a military context, the OODA loop has become a popular decision-making model for a diverse array of individuals and organizations.

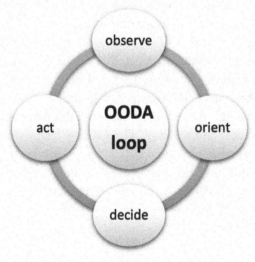

OBSERVE: Rapidly build an accurate picture of the situation at hand. What are the facts? Who are the main players? What information is essential? What information is missing? What information is irrelevant?

ORIENT: Analyze the information gathered during the observation phase to establish context, create clarity, and hone a point of view. What options are available? What's the desired end state?

DECIDE: Determine a specific course of action based on synthesizing the data points from observing and orienting. Develop a theory. Test assumptions. Make clear choices. Define the path forward.

ACT: Implement an action plan with speed and precision.

For Boyd, tempo is key to optimizing the OODA loop. If your team makes sound decisions faster than your opponents, you can potentially disrupt their decision-making cycle as they constantly react to yours.

In Boyd's words, "The ability to operate at a faster tempo or rhythm than an adversary enables one to fold the adversary back inside himself so that he can neither appreciate nor keep up with what is going on."[173]

As a strategist, you must have a reliable, ever-improving system for decision-making. The OODA loop is one possibility. Plenty of others exist too.

Don't hold out on the hope of finding the perfect decision-making model. Pick the ones that work best for you in a given context and keep improving them.

ONE-WAY VS. TWO-WAY DOORS

Not all decisions are the same in terms of consequence and finality.

Some decisions are reversible or changeable. Other decisions are irreversible or unchangeable. This distinction may sound obvious on paper. In practice, though, not enough individuals and organizations think and operate in this way.

For Amazon, this distinction represents a key strategy in their overall decision-making architecture.[174] Bezos defines irreversible decisions as one-way doors: If you walk through and don't like what you see on the other side, you can't return to where you came from.[174] That's why one-way door decisions "must be made methodically, carefully, slowly, with great deliberation and consultation."[176]

Bezos describes reversible decisions as two-way doors: If you walk through and don't like what you see on the other side, you can return to where you came from. Since these decisions are changeable, you should make them faster and with less hierarchy involved.

Organizations suffer, according to Bezos, when they treat both types of decision as the same. Or, worse yet, when they apply the one-way door methodology to two-way door decisions. Doing the latter results in "slowness, unthoughtful risk aversion, failure to experiment sufficiently, and consequently diminished invention."[177]

As a strategist, you must develop a knack for distinguishing between one-way and two-way door decisions and managing each effectively.

AN APP FOR THAT

Decisions carry a variety of inputs.

Speed: Some decisions should be made faster than others.

Clarity: Some decisions include more background information than others.

Stakes: Some decisions result in greater consequences than others.

Engagement: Some decisions demand a more egalitarian approach than others.

Transparency: Some decisions have a more public profile than others.

The consulting firm NOBL created an app called The Decider to help decision-makers discern how decision inputs influence decision outputs. After a user answers a handful of questions regarding the inputs associated with a desired decision, The Decider app recommends a decision framework—along a continuum of eight decision models—to assist them in their decision-making process.

The Decider app is a forcing function. It forces you to take a step back, lean into a deliberative mindset, acknowledge the multiple inputs associated with a decision, calibrate the nature and scope of these inputs, and then determine how these inputs will shape your outputs.

Sure, you may not need yet another app in your life. But you surely need a deliberate process for discerning how decision inputs shape decision outputs.

THE STRATEGIST

Being a strategist means being regularly tested on your decision-making abilities. Accept the reality that your decisions are held to a higher degree of scrutiny because everyone expects you to be a paragon of good judgment. Rather than fear this fact, use it to your advantage.

Keep a log of your decisions and rate them according to Grant's matrix. Break down your decisions to figure out why your process was shallow and how it could have been deepened. Or consider what made a particular decision process deep and try to repeat it.

When a strategist is wrong, they strive to improve their decision-making process with the goal of not repeating the misstep. When a non-strategist is wrong, they deflect and blame.

If the strategist is wrong once, the non-strategist is wrong twice.

STRATEGIST'S NOTEBOOK

LESS WRONG

Designing the right idea. Making the right decision. Acting at the right moment. Seizing the right opportunity. Delivering the right result. Being right is deeply satisfying.

And that makes being wrong unsatisfying and hard to take. Nobody feels more pressure to be constantly right—and, by extension, not even remotely wrong—than strategists.

No organization wants to spend time, resources, and reputational capital or incur opportunity costs moving in the wrong direction based on the wrong strategy. And no strategist wants to be responsible for leading their organization astray. Given this immense pressure to be right, it makes sense why strategists would fear being wrong.

But this fear can lead to disastrous results if left unchecked.

The fear of being wrong may prompt you to search fervently for more reasons why you're right. This impulse leaves you susceptible to confirmation bias: You see only what you expect to see in building your evidence base. Or to desirability bias: You see only what you want to see. Or to the spotlight effect: You see only what's visible to you and presume it's the total picture.

In each case, the fear of being wrong can make you, ironically, even more likely to be wrong in the end. As the strategist Steven Johnson observes, "Sometimes the easiest way to be wrong is to be certain you are right."[178]

STRATEGIES FOR RETHINKING

What if you could rethink the whole notion of being wrong? What if you could transform this negative fear into a positive capability? What if you developed strategies for being less wrong? And by doing so, what if you could increase your odds of being right?

If rethinking your relationship to being wrong were a journey, there's no better guide than Adam Grant's *Think Again: The Power of Knowing What You Don't Know.*[179]

For Grant, one of the best strategies for curbing your ways of being wrong is to rethink your default behavior. Grant believes many people spend their days role-playing a mixture of three professions: preacher, prosecutor, and politician.

You slip into preacher mode when you justify the rightness of your ideas. You shift into prosecutor mode when you try to prove why the other person is wrong in their thinking. And you morph into politician mode when you want to win over others to your position. All three mindsets are problematic, asserts Grant, because they hold you back from rethinking your own views. The better strategy?

SCIENTIST MODE

If you want to excel at rethinking and therefore lessen your ways of being wrong, Grant recommends behaving like a scientist. The scientist's job is to be acutely aware of knowing what they don't know. Their hunches and theories must be tested to survive another round of testing, analyzing, and scrutiny—and another one after that.

They think in order to rethink. That is why, in Grant's words, they refuse to let their ideas slide into ideologies. Most importantly, they genuinely search for reasons why they might be wrong.

Scientists live by the logic of Grant's four-part cycle for rethinking: humility, doubt, curiosity, and discovery.[180] They also steer clear of his cycle for overconfidence: pride, conviction, confirmation and desirability bias, and validation.[181] In short, if you want to decrease your chances of being wrong, permanently shift your mindset to scientist mode—and leave the blind spots of the preacher, prosecutor, and politician roles behind you.

LEVELS OF CONFIDENCE

One of the best ways to make these rethinking habits stick is to upgrade your conception of being right and wrong. Most people think of being right or wrong in categorical terms: You are either 100 percent right or 100 percent wrong.

In turn, once they make up their mind on a particular issue, they rarely revisit their decision prior to rendering it. Why? "If our only options are being 100% right or 100% wrong, with nothing in between, then information that potentially contradicts a belief requires a total downgrade, from right all the way to wrong," notes Annie Duke.[182]

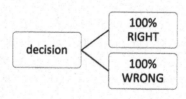

And since most people interpret being all wrong as undermining their positive self-image, their self-serving bias prompts them to ignore or downplay disconfirming information.[183]

The best decision-makers, by contrast, think in levels of confidence.

They say, for instance, they have an 80 percent chance of being right on a particular issue. Then they analyze confirming and disconfirming information to upgrade their thinking and adjust their estimate up or down. A hidden advantage to probabilistic thinking is its ability to force you to simultaneously calibrate your likelihood of being wrong.

In the example above, there is a 20 percent chance of being wrong. The simple act of acknowledging your probability of being wrong helps demystify it. Your chances of being wrong should be effectively measured, managed, and mitigated, not crudely feared.

Consider the concept of failing fast and cheap. The idea is straightforward: Companies should quickly discover what's not working with a prototype so they can promptly pivot to developing a better solution.

This methodology is grounded in the logic that being wrong is a critical step on the journey to being right. In other words, the aim is to be wrong faster and cheaper in order to be right sooner, longer, and with greater value.

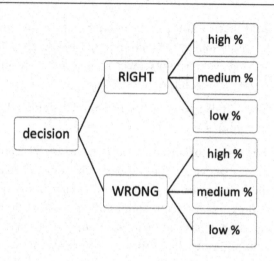

Strategists must adopt a similar mindset. Being wrong can be the key to unlocking a higher level of confidence in being right.

Don't succumb to the pressure of always trying to have the right answer or make the right call. This disposition can easily lead to sloppy thinking, including a total absence of rethinking. Overconfidence in being right can be deadly on many levels. As the saying goes, "It's the strong swimmers who often drown."

As a strategist, think in levels of confidence. Rethink the ways you could be wrong. Edit your beliefs. Upgrade your opinions. Replace whether-or-not (only two) choices with which-one (more than two) options. And get comfortable with what you don't know. Grant says it best: "If knowledge is power, knowing what we don't know is wisdom."[184]

While others are preoccupied with being more and more right, strategists focus on being less wrong.

THINK TWICE

The writer Natalie Goldberg believes writers live twice.[185] They experience the world with the rest of society. Then they return to their desk and vividly bring these details to life a second time via their writing.

Strategists do the same. They experience meetings, presentations, and discussions with the rest of the organization. Then they replay these details over and over again to test and retest the thinking around the room.

Everybody thinks once. Strategists think twice.

MESSAGE BETTER

Try this experiment: Don't think of an elephant. What are you thinking of right now? An elephant. Why? When you negate a frame, explains the linguist George Lakoff, you simultaneously evoke it.[186] In other words, once the image of an elephant is triggered, you can't help but have it lingering in your head.

Welcome to the world of framing.

What is framing? Imagine framing as a movie screen in your mind. When language is framed one way, the picture is perfect, and the dialogue is obvious. Your brain processes the information quickly and easily. That's effective framing.

When language is framed a different way, the picture is grainy, and the dialogue requires subtitles. Your brain must work harder to compute. That's ineffective framing.

Since the brain favors quick and easy solutions, effective framing tends to capture the attention and support of most people.

Why does framing matter? Selecting the right frames is critical to building the right message. And having the right message is essential to launching the right strategy. If you can't convince others that your strategy deserves their attention and support, your ideas—no matter how promising—won't take flight.

Think of it this way: Strategy is less bought and more sold. You have to persuade others to act by converting listeners to believers and then believers to owners.

Where do you start? Work backward. If you want others to embrace your strategy, offer up a powerful message. If you want to build a powerful message, craft the best frames. If you want to craft the best frames, study the nuances of priming and coding.

PRIMING

Priming occurs when one stimulus, below conscious awareness, influences your thoughts and behaviors on another stimulus. Here are five examples of priming:

Example 1: Word Association

If you encounter the word EAT, you are more likely to complete the word fragment SO_P as SOUP than as SOAP.[187] Why? Since your mind associates the term eat with the notion of food, you are primed to think of soup faster than soap. Alternatively, if you encounter the word WASH, you are more likely to complete the word fragment SO_P as SOAP than as SOUP.

Example 2: Contextual Association

When asked to support a levy for school funding, voters were significantly more likely to do so when the polling station was housed in a school as opposed to another location.[188] Why? The polling location at the school primed their thinking to be more receptive to a levy that benefited schools.

Example 3: Ordering Association

A study assigned character traits to two hypothetical individuals represented as Individual A and Individual B.[189] Participants were asked to read a list of character traits for each and share their impression of the two individuals.

Individual A: intelligent—industrious—impulsive—critical—stubborn—envious

Individual B: envious—stubborn—critical—impulsive—industrious—intelligent

Though the traits for each individual were exactly the same, most participants viewed Individual A more favorably than Individual B. Why?

The ordering of words influences their subsequent interpretation. Since the term intelligent has a positive connotation, the words that follow seem less objectionable for Individual A. By contrast, since the term envious has a negative connotation, the words that follow seem more problematic for Individual B.

Example 4: Sentiment Association

Two different hand sanitizers are for sale. The price, size, content, and efficacy are the same for both. The only difference is the description on the bottle. Brand X says it kills 98 percent of germs. Brand Y says only 2 percent of germs survive.

Why do most people choose Brand X over Brand Y? When it comes to germs, you attribute a positive sentiment to killing them and a negative one to allowing them to survive. Most people prefer positive connotations.

Similarly, imagine you need a surgical procedure done. Doctor A describes the surgery as having an 80 percent success rate. Doctor B describes this same surgery as having a 20 percent failure rate.

Why do most people say yes to Doctor A and no to Doctor B—even though they reference the same surgical procedure? Since the 80 percent option is framed in a positive light, it proves more persuasive to most decision-makers.

Example 5: Comparative Association

You get to choose your annual income. Do you want $100,000 or $50,000? Dumb question, right? How surprised are you that 50 percent of survey respondents were asked this question and picked $50,000?[190]

The individuals were subjected to a comparative association. They were told they could earn $100,000 as long as their peers earned double that amount. Or they could earn $50,000 as long as their peers earned half that amount. The reason half of the individuals chose significantly less money in absolute terms is that they wanted better standing amongst their peers in relative terms.

CODING

The former child psychiatrist Clotaire Rapaille believes the first time you hear a word a mental imprint is formed.[191] This code stays with you—mostly at an unconscious level—and subtly influences your subsequent associations.

After delivering a lecture on his coding theory in the 1970s, one of the parents of Rapaille's students suggested he share his insights with Nestlé. The company had been trying to sell instant coffee in Japan and was failing miserably. After immersing himself in the culture, Rapaille realized Japanese people had no mental imprint or code for coffee because tea had dominated nearly every aspect of Japanese life for centuries.

Instead of trying to convince Japanese adults to choose coffee over tea, Rapaille recommended Nestlé spend its time and resources creating a positive imprint for coffee within Japanese culture. To this end, Nestlé started selling coffee-flavored candy and desserts aimed at Japanese preteens.

A few years later, they introduced a customized version of coffee for these then-teenagers. And a few years after that, they reintroduced their instant coffee in Japan. This time, their once-unpopular coffee enjoyed considerable success.

By creating a positive code for coffee for a new generation of Japanese consumers, argues Rapaille, Nestlé had built the desire and demand it would then supply.

Rapaille has spent the last thirty years helping companies decipher the coding behind consumer choices. His advice is straightforward: If your idea or product resonates with the code in the consumer's mind, it has a far better chance of succeeding.

Howard Schultz seems to have intuitively understood the power of coding when he founded Starbucks. He envisioned Starbucks to be this "third place" between home and work that would offer customers a sense of connection and belonging.[192] Believing these deeply ingrained human values were absent from traditional retail, Schultz wanted Starbucks to embody them at every turn.

For employees, Starbucks was among the first private US companies to provide comprehensive health insurance to part-time workers.[193] *Belonging.* For customers, Starbucks allowed them to customize their orders as a matter of course, resulting in 170,000 variations of Starbucks beverages.[194] And the cup donned their name. *Connection.*

Connection and belonging are the codes. Coffee is the product.

FRAMING

Both priming and coding give you a sense of the powerful yet unspoken forces at play in framing. Much of framing's magic is rooted in the notion of prospect theory developed by the psychologist and Nobel Prize winner Daniel Kahneman.[195]

According to Kahneman, individuals view most situations in terms of potential losses or potential gains. Since more mental weight and significance are ascribed to a loss than to an equivalent gain, most individuals try hard to avoid losses. This loss aversion, in turn, makes them more inclined to side with positive frames connoting gains and progress.

MAKING WORDS COUNT

One of the most well-known examples of framing, or in this case reframing, is the term estate tax. Republicans had long wanted this tax eliminated, yet they couldn't persuade others to see it their way. In the early 2000s, the political strategist Frank Luntz convinced Republican leaders to start framing the issue as a death tax.

Calling it an estate tax seemed to cater to elites, recounts Luntz, which made most Americans uninterested in reducing or eliminating it.[196] Framing it as a death tax, on the other hand, made it seem unfair and untimely to a broader cross section of Americans.

Families, in Luntz's words, "should not be further burdened at the most difficult time of their lives."[197] The majority of Americans agreed with Luntz's logic and supported the subsequent legislative action to reduce it.

Companies also tap the power of framing. When Schultz returned to lead Starbucks in 2008, he claimed the company had lost its way. His primary focus was to reframe the core message: "Starbucks is not a coffee company that serves people. It is a people company that serves coffee."[198]

Framing is a subtle but significant way for organizations to shape the narrative that surrounds them. Notice how Airbnb talks about belonging, not lodging. Nike talks about inspiration, not products. Amazon talks about customers, not logistics. Walmart talks about living better, not merely saving money. Coca-Cola talks about optimism, not soft drinks. Facebook talks about community and connections, not technology.

How is your organization laddering up its messaging to a better vantage point?

MAKING NUMBERS STICK

In *Making Numbers Count: The Art and Science of Communicating Numbers*, Chip Heath and Karla Starr claim most people unwittingly pick the wrong frames when communicating numbers.[199] They try to explain one number by pointing to more numbers. Such doubling down on quantitative framing tends to create more confusion, not less.

For Heath and Starr, the solution is simple: If you want numbers to stick, you must translate them into human experience. You must use clear, concrete, and compelling words to bring your numbers to life.

For example, almost annually, a politician calls for eliminating the National Endowment for the Arts (NEA) to purportedly save money for the federal government. Here's a traditional framing of the situation: the NEA's budget in 2016 was $148 million and represented only 0.004 percent of the overall federal budget. Here's an alternative framing by Heath and Starr: "Trying to balance the budget by eliminating the NEA would be like editing a 90,000-word novel by eliminating 4 words."[200] Which frame sticks with you?

What's the difference between a millionaire and a billionaire? Here's a traditional framing of the situation: a billionaire is one thousand times richer than a millionaire. Here's an alternative framing by Heath and Starr: a million seconds is twelve days from now, while a billion seconds is thirty-two years.[201] Which frame sticks with you?

Heath and Starr offer dozens of useful examples of how to translate numbers into easy-to-understand human experiences. Given the central role numbers can play in strategy work, every strategist should make framing numbers a key skill to hone.

THE STRATEGIST

Better frames lead to better messaging. And better messaging gives your strategy better odds of sticking, persuading, spreading, and succeeding.

As a strategist, you must be a student of messaging.

Study the anatomy behind great messages. What frames are chosen, and why? What frames are excluded, and why? Is priming or coding involved?

On the flip side, collect examples of bad messaging. Where did they miss the mark, and why? What better frames could have been used at the time?

The best messages do two things: they stick, and they spread.

A great primer on how to craft sticky messages is *Made to Stick: Why Some Ideas Survive and Others Die* by Chip Heath and Dan Heath.[202] An excellent read on how to generate viral content is *Contagious: Why Things Catch On* by Jonah Berger.[203] Both are must-read books for strategists wanting to upgrade their messaging game.

As you hone your skills in building great messages, keep these five insights top of mind:

1 **Don't allow framing to be dismissed as spin doctoring.** Linguists will tell you every message you encounter is always already framed. Therefore, the question you must never fail to ask is straightforward: Are you going to accept the inherited frame or change it?

2 **Test your frames with smaller groups before sharing them with a larger audience.** Figure out which frames bring your strategy to life the most by giving it a sense of feel, novelty, resonance, and positivity. Remember this: A bad frame can ruin a great strategy.

3 **If you have the ability to choose where to position your best frames, situate them at the beginning and end of your message.** Research shows people remember beginnings and endings better than the rest.

4 **Once you curate your best frames, repeat them over and over and over again.** Robert Zajonc's research shows individuals develop a clear preference for things familiar to them—a psychological theory known as the mere exposure effect.[204]

5 **Accept that framing can be used in improper and dishonest ways too.** Don't do it to others, and don't allow others to do it to you. The aim of framing is to persuade, not deceive.

In the end, if naysayers repeat your frames in negative ways, don't panic. Just recall Lakoff's elephant. Every time the naysayers try to negate your frame, they keep it lingering in everyone's mind for longer.

STRATEGIST'S NOTEBOOK

FUTURE PRESS RELEASE

Before any Amazon team pursues a new product, service, or initiative, they must write a future press release. As the name suggests, the announcement is set in the future. It presupposes the new idea has already been active and successful in the market for several months or years. The press release tells its origin story.

Ian McAllister, a former Amazon leader, describes the component parts of a future press release as follows:

Heading: Names the product in a way the customer understands.

Sub-Heading: Defines the main benefit of the product to the customer.

Summary: Elaborates on the customer, the product, and the benefits.

Problem: Explains the problem to be solved.

Solution: Describes how the product solves the problem.

Team Quote: Captures the customer-first approach to the process.

How to Get Started: Details how easy it is to get started.

Customer Quote: Captures the desired experience in the customer's words.

Call to Action: Specifies the next step to take.[205]

A future press release is designed to wow, not bore. To keep it clear and crisp, aim for one to two pages. McAllister suggests using Oprah-speak: "Imagine you're sitting on Oprah's couch and have just explained the product to her, and then you listen as she explains it to her audience."[206] The upshot: simple sells; complex confounds.

If the press release proves hard to write, it's probably a good sign your idea needs more work, notes McAllister. And reshaping a hypothetical press release is much cheaper and faster than iterating a real product or service.

For John Rossman, a future press release is a forcing function at Amazon: "Once the press release is reviewed and approved, teams should have a very difficult time backing out of the commitments they have made."[207] Rossman continues, "A leader can refer to parts of the press release and use it to remind and hold teams accountable. It paints a clear vision to galvanize understanding and commitment. It is a contract."[208]

Strategists know the distinct advantages of crafting a future press release.

First, it forces your team to commit to a narrative explanation of the who, why, what, and how of a new idea. Rather than glossing over critical details via a verbal or slide presentation, the narrative-based press release rightly places a premium on choices, clarity, framing, and attention to detail.

Second, a future press release forces your team to capitalize on backcasting: a planning method whereby you define a future end point and then work backward to determine what actions are needed to bridge your current means to your desired end.

The strategists David Yoffie and Michael Cusumano describe this time-traveling technique as looking forward and reasoning back: "Part game theorist and part chess master, great strategists 'look forward' to determine where they want their companies to be at a given point in the future and then 'reason back' to identify moves that will take the business there."[209]

Finally, a future press release forces your team to agree on a shared vision and then presumably carry forward this alignment through the development and implementation phases, guarding against scope creep or misalignment.

INNOVATE BETTER

The pressure for organizations to do things smarter, faster, and better is intense. It's also here to stay. Innovation has become more of a vital need than a fleeting want.

Your job as a strategist is to keep asking an upstream question: How does your organization get more innovative in its approach to innovation?

Duleesha Kulasooriya is a futurist who spends his days forecasting trends in technology, innovation, and strategy. Getting more innovative about innovation has long captured Kulasooriya's attention. In his view, too many organizations fail at breakthrough innovation because they try to innovate from the inside out rather than from the outside in.[210]

When organizations try to innovate from the inside out, they typically succumb to the "institutional antibodies" that attack change.[211] How do these antibodies work? The risks get overstated. The cost gets overestimated. Complexity gets overinflated. And doubt gets overblown. The net result? Innovation takes a back seat to the comfort of staying with the status quo.

Kulasooriya, therefore, advocates for an outside-in approach to innovation.[212] It hinges on situating innovation work on the edge of your organization, scaling it to success, and then using these upside benefits to reinvent the core.

DEFINE THE EDGE

The edge is a highly creative environment set apart from an organization's core structures and central processes.

Importantly, the edge is established away from the organization's main physical home—in a different building, town, or state. The edge's distance from the core is designed to keep innovation work as far away from the institutional antibodies as possible.

The chief product officer at Adobe, Scott Belsky, believes the edge unlocks an atypical mindset: "Innovation and entrepreneurship happen at the edge of reason, because it is finding something that is unreasonable to most. Otherwise it would have been done."[213]

BUILD THE EDGE

Having secured a dedicated place for edge activities away from your core, now it's time to build your innovation agenda. Here are four lessons from Kulasooriya to keep top of mind when innovating from the outside in:

1. **Edge innovation should be defined as new or different.** Make it abundantly clear to everyone involved that your edge efforts don't compete with your organization's core products or services. Your edge work is ancillary, extra, and experimental. It's the definition of low risk.

2. **Edge innovation should be funded with minimal resources from the core.** Kulasooriya advocates for "starving the edge" by forcing the team to secure funding from other sources and partners beyond the core.[214] The aim of imposing constraints—such as limited resources and self-sufficiency—is to compel the edge team to be as lean, scrappy, focused, networked, and, above all, effective as possible.

3. **Edge innovation should be speedy.** If the core's normal build time for a new initiative is two to three

years, the edge should strive for results in six to nine months. Such a tight time frame for innovating serves multiple aims. It keeps the team intensely focused on results, not activities. It forces the team to solicit feedback sooner in the build process. And it allows the team to pull the plug easier and faster on a mediocre build since there are less sunken costs, red tape, and hurt egos to address.

4 **Edge innovation should be scalable.** Your goal is to produce game-changing outcomes, not incremental improvements. You want your edge innovation to be so powerful and promising that incorporating it into your organization's core seems like a no-brainer.

As Kulasooriya explains, "As the edge scales and becomes more integral to the organization as a whole, the old core must eventually transform to continue capitalizing on the opportunity. Ultimately, a 'new core' will supersede the old with distinct practices and capabilities to maximize the upside potential of the edge."[215] Migrating your scaled solution from the edge back to the core is central to the outside-in approach to innovation.

Perhaps the biggest advantage to innovating on the edge of your organization is the ability to outmaneuver the institutional antibodies that haunt the core. By the time your breakthrough innovation is ready to move from the edge to the core, it has had too much success and momentum to be derailed by the naysayers.

EDGE EXEMPLARS

Some of today's most innovative companies have been scaling the edge for years.

In 1981, Steve Jobs moved a small team of creatives, whom he affectionately called pirates, out of Apple's main office building and into a leased space down the street next to a Texaco gas station.[216] Jobs charged this team with building the first Macintosh computer at this off-site location known fondly as Texaco Towers. If asked to explain this edge group, Jobs would say: "It's better to be a pirate than to join the navy."[217]

In 2004, Amazon had a vision to improve the physical book. A small team accepted the challenge and moved into a shared space in a Palo Alto law library, more than 800 miles away from Amazon's headquarters. Within three years of establishing this edge group, Amazon launched its first e-reader, called Kindle. This edge team, known as Amazon Lab126, became a powerhouse for innovation, research, and development, building other signature products such as Amazon Fire Tablets, Amazon Fire TV, and Amazon Echo.

In 2009, Microsoft established The Garage, a dedicated space for their employees, customers, and ecosystem to "drive collaboration, creativity, and experimentation."[218]

In 2010, Google established X, a moonshot factory for long-term projects designed to solve the world's hardest problems.[219] Located outside the Googleplex, X became an independent Alphabet company in 2015.

More recently, a growing number of companies have established innovation centers at major research universities or within innovation districts. Their edge investments are a clear vote in favor of an outside-in approach to innovation.

Beyond surveying organizations that have successfully gotten more innovative about innovation, it's worth studying ones that have failed too. And perhaps none are more notable than Kodak.

KODAK: COLLAPSING IN SLOW MOTION

Kodak was founded in 1892. For multiple decades, Kodak ranked among the world's most successful companies. During the 1970s, they sold 90 percent of the film and 85 percent of the cameras in America. In 1996, Kodak was valued at $28 billion and had 140,000 employees. By 2012, the one-time titan was bankrupt.

Kodak's inability to change with the times and adapt to a digital world is a cautionary tale most innovators have heard, if not repeated.

But did you know that the world's first digital camera was invented by—wait for it—a Kodak engineer named Steve Sasson? Yes, that's right. The specific technology that sunk Kodak is the same technology Sasson first invented in 1976—in a Kodak laboratory. He demonstrated this technology to Kodak's leadership that same year.

How could Kodak collapse in seemingly slow motion?

It's tempting to assume Kodak was utterly uninterested in the fast-changing world around them. But the facts suggest otherwise. Kodak had invested billions in developing a range of digital technologies. They had even acquired a photo-sharing site in 2001—well before Facebook was founded in 2004.[220]

Their fundamental failure, as Scott Anthony observes, was in treating digital as a side bet for too long: "Where they failed was in realizing that online photo sharing *was* the new business, not just a way to expand the printing business."[221]

Imagine if Kodak had instead adopted the strategy of innovating from the outside in.

They could have positioned Sasson and a small team of creatives on the edge of the organization, away from the institutional antibodies that eventually buried his idea. They could have compelled him to get better and faster feedback from outside the organization. And they could have helped him scale his new digital technology so that the core had no choice but to accept it.

In this alternative history, the digital camera could have been Kodak's signature strength rather than its Achilles heel.

The strategist Peter Diamandis offers another insightful take on Kodak's collapse.[222] For him, Kodak not only missed the domination of the digital camera but also the massive desire to capture and share memories in a fast, easy, and extensive way. Enter Instagram.

Instagram rapidly became *the* place to document one's digital life. If the old "Kodak Moment" belonged to Kodak, as Diamandis observes, the new "Kodak Moment" belongs to Instagram. In 2012, only three months after Kodak filed for bankruptcy, Instagram was sold to Facebook for $1 billion. The company was all of eighteen months old and had only thirteen employees.

In Diamandis's words, "Instead of using their weighty position to corner the market, they [Kodak] were instead cornered by the market."[223]

THE STRATEGIST

As a strategist, you must be willing and able to articulate the advantages of an outside-in approach to innovation. There's a reason Apple, Amazon, Google, Microsoft, and a slew of other companies have moved innovation to the edge.

It represents their best opportunity to get more innovative about innovation.

Perhaps the novelist Kurt Vonnegut describes the edge best: "Out on the edge you see all kinds of things you can't see from the center.... Big, undreamed-of things—the people on the edge see them first."[224]

STRATEGIST'S NOTEBOOK

NEW YORK TO NEW MEXICO

Strategy is not painting by numbers, following directions, or memorizing the map. And it's not cut and paste. It's training yourself to think differently about everything—obstacles, opportunities, and optionality.

Strategy is an unmistakably creative endeavor.

Imagine you are told to travel from New York to New Mexico.

In Scenario A, you're given an abundance of time, money, and technology.

With these resources in place, your choices are easy to identify and execute. From your smartphone, you can book a plane, train, or rental car. Once confirmed, you receive detailed information via your handheld device on where to go and what to do. From there, you simply follow the instructions and end up in New Mexico.

In Scenario B, your time, money, and technology are all compromised.

You have twenty dollars to spend, forty-eight hours to get there, and no access to a smartphone. Oh, by the way, your career depends on making it to New Mexico on time and within budget. With these unusual conditions in place, your next steps are anything but obvious.

These two scenarios dramatize the difference between planning and strategizing.

Planning is predictable. You choose from a clear-cut menu of options, follow the rules, and the desired outcome typically materializes.

Strategizing, by contrast, is unpredictable. You assemble not-so-obvious means and find creative ways to leverage them for your preferred ends. The effort is soaked in uncertainty, improvisation, resilience, and risk.

In planning, you see ahead—to the next step. In strategizing, you see beyond—to the horizon. The latter takes imagination and ingenuity—as well as some luck—to get there.

Strategy professor Adam Bradenburger believes in the inextricable connection between strategy and creativity. Game-changing strategies, in his words, "are born of creative thinking: a spark of intuition, a connection between different ways of thinking, a leap into the unexpected."[225] Bradenburger encourages other strategy professors to teach their students "how to be creative and rigorous at the same time."[226]

Strategy professor Richard Rumelt agrees, "You don't 'pick' a strategy; you create it."[227] For Rumelt, strategy is never a matter of simply picking winning ideas from a set of prepackaged choices. Strategic choices must be first imagined, constructed, and curated before they are molded into strategic actions.

COACH BETTER

Every organization needs a well-crafted people strategy. And every strategist needs to help their organization build a strategic direction to get there. Where do you start?

Strategists thrive on coaching, both getting and giving. If you want to grow more and better strategists, you must be able to create, sustain, and scale a culture of coaching across the enterprise. In the process, you must never lose sight of the importance of team and talent.

TEAM

Building a team is different than hiring talent. There's no better example of this axiom than the 2004 USA men's Olympic basketball team. This team had twelve NBA players, including perennial all-stars Tim Duncan and Allen Iverson; budding stars Lebron James, Carmelo Anthony, and Dwayne Wade; and future Hall of Fame coach Larry Brown.

Despite having a roster stacked with outstanding professional players from the NBA, the world's best basketball league by a wide margin at the time, the team lost three games in the 2004 Olympics. Their bronze-medal finish ended a twenty-four-game winning streak and a run of three consecutive gold medals for Team USA since 1992.

Reflecting on this shocking disappointment, Coach Mike Krzyzewski recalls the biggest lesson learned from the collapse: the USA Basketball organization had lost its way by harboring the misguided belief that assembling great talent equates to building a great team.[228] Coach K agreed to lead Team USA following the 2004 debacle and subscribed to a simple tenet: "Team over talent."[229]

With this team-over-talent strategy in full display, Coach K restored USA's dominance with Olympic gold medals in 2008, 2012, and 2016.

Every time you hear a leader say their people strategy is to hire great people and get out of the way, think of the 2004 Olympic team. Having great talent is not the same as building a great team. Overestimating the capacity of inputs can lead to subpar outputs.

In building your people strategy, your organization must have something definitive to say about teamwork. For a direct and unique take on teamwork, check out Netflix's manifesto on culture and people.[230]

Here Netflix spells out its definition of a dream team. It explains what it is and, importantly, what it isn't. It also draws a clear distinction between being a team and being a family: "We model ourselves on being a team, not a family. A family is about unconditional love, despite, say, your siblings' bad behavior. A dream team is about pushing yourself to be the best teammate you can be, caring intensely about your teammates, and knowing that you may not be on the team forever."[231]

As its cofounder Reed Hastings details, Netflix likens its strategy to a professional sports team.[232] The company believes every position must be filled by the best player, that each team member must play at a high level to keep their respective position, and that nobody is safe from being cut from the team, including Hastings.

As a strategist, you must push your organization to define teamwork. What is it? Why is it important? How will you know when it's working or not? Does your organization want to own the identity of a team or a family? If your organization identifies as a team, does it operate with the same heightened levels of accountability as a professional sports team?

TALENT

Favoring team over talent doesn't mean the latter is irrelevant. Far from it. Every winning team has talent at its core. A sound people strategy, therefore, should have something to say about talent, too.

What kind of talent does your organization need to thrive? What kind of talent doesn't work for your purposes?

This last question comes from Netflix. The company's "no brilliant jerks" strategy is built on the unapologetic decision that jerks—no matter their intellect or efficacy—have no place in their organization. In its cofounder's words, "The cost of jerkiness to effective teamwork is too high. Jerks are likely to rip your organization apart from the inside."[233]

The "keeper test" is another Netflix strategy for assessing talent. Supervisors are trained to routinely ask: "If a person on your team were to quit tomorrow, would you try to change their mind? Or would you accept their resignation, perhaps with a little relief?"[234] For Netflix, the latter response is a clear sign the supervisor should manage the employee out of the organization right away and replace them with a star who the supervisor would be willing to fight to keep.[235]

As a strategist, you must force your organization to speak in the language of choice when it comes to talent. What type of talent do you choose to recruit? What type of talent do you choose to retain? What type of talent will you not tolerate—your version of the "no brilliant jerks" choice?

COACHING

While nearly every organization talks about talent, fewer have put pen to paper to detail the criticality of teamwork. And fewer still have anything substantive to say about coaching.

If organizations pursue coaching, it typically follows one of two paths: the big fix or the heir apparent.

In the first path, after learning that a leader exhibits questionable behavior, an organization hires an external coach to fix the problem. Though the engagement is intended to be a positive step, the process can feel punitive to the individual involved.

In the second path, after identifying a promising leader they want to grow and develop, an organization hires an external coach to enhance, expand, and accelerate the individual's professional development. Far from punitive, this scenario can be viewed by others as highly privileged, as one handpicked leader enjoys the benefits of professional help while their peers have to figure it out for themselves.

For both the big fix and the heir apparent, the coaching experience is isolated to the individual, episodic in frequency, brief in duration, and highly selective in its impact. It's no wonder this type of coaching can garner a bad rap.

But there's another way.

If you're unfamiliar with the name Bill Campbell, don't fret.

Until his death in 2016, Campbell maintained a relatively low profile, despite his day job of coaching some of the biggest names in business. No less than Steve Jobs, Larry Page, Eric Schmidt, Sheryl Sandberg, Sundar Pichai, and Susan Wojcicki—in addition to several other titans of technology—called Campbell their professional coach.

In *Trillion Dollar Coach: The Leadership Playbook of Silicon Valley's Bill Campbell*, Eric Schmidt brings Campbell's coaching philosophy to life. Campbell's mantra is simple: You can't be a great leader without also being a great coach.[236]

Campbell coached these superstars to reach their full potential by training them to become coaches in their own right. He taught them to never stop coaching—themselves, their teams, and their organizations.

Campbell's coaching philosophy is deliberate and systematic. If every leader in your organization is expected to coach, both getting and giving, coaching can no longer be treated as selective, sporadic, or short-lived. It can no longer be viewed as punitive or privileged.

Instead, coaching becomes pervasive and persistent. Coaching is then woven into the cultural fabric of your organization.

Campbell's mantra is perfectly suited for strategists, too: You can't be a great strategist without also being a great coach. Being a strategist is a two-way street. You must be able to receive coaching, and you must be able to provide coaching. With this interplay of getting and giving, coaching becomes a habit that is all-encompassing.

For a useful analogy, consider Olympians and professional athletes. They represent the best of the best in their respective sport. They have mastered the ins and outs of their domain to an extraordinary degree. By any measure, they possess enough knowledge, skills, and motivation to guide themselves. And yet, all of them rely on coaches, season after season.

Why the need for coaches at this apex level? Even for the best professionals, coaches have the ability to bring out the best in them—to elevate their game to heights they could not achieve on their own. If these world-class professionals still need constant coaching, why don't you and your organization?

One of the biggest obstacles to creating a culture of coaching is the misguided assumption that coaching must be professionalized. True, professionals who coach others for a living often have formal credentials and training to their name. But that's a choice, not a requirement.

There's no legal body or central authority that controls who can or can't coach. At its core, coaching is about helping others become better versions of themselves. You don't need permission or validation from a third party to do just that.

How do you become an effective coach?

Fortunately, the literature on coaching is vast and varied. You can read the writings of highly accomplished executive coaches, such as Marshall Goldsmith or John Mattone. You can study the habits of legendary sports coaches, such as Mike Krzyzewski or Pat Summitt. Or you can explore a range of digital resources from numerous coaching associations, such as The International Coach Federation (ICF) or The Center for Credentialing and Education (CCE).

If you want an easy, accessible inroad to learning about coaching, Michael Bungay Stanier's *The Coaching Habit: Say Less, Ask More & Change the Way You Lead Forever* is a good place to start.[237] The author defines seven essential questions that enable you to create and sustain a viable coaching environment.

To help organize and structure your coaching conversations, Stanier suggests using the 3P framework: projects, people, and patterns.

Project coaching tends to focus on processes and performance. People coaching tends to focus on conflict and relationships. Pattern coaching tends to focus on self-awareness and development. The key is to figure out which type of conversation is needed for a given context.

THE STRATEGIST

Every organization has a people strategy—whether they know it or not. The ineffective ones happen by default; the effective ones happen by design.

In designing your people strategy, here are some questions to consider:

1. How are you defining the role and responsibilities of teamwork?
2. What type of behavior will not be tolerated?
3. What constitutes your keeper test?
4. What investments are you making to create and sustain a culture of coaching?
5. How are you rewarding good coaches?

Organizations routinely underestimate the importance of having a sound people strategy. It takes a strategist to unveil the obvious: Every single strategy your organization pursues wins or loses based on the performance of your people.

STRATEGIST'S NOTEBOOK

THE IKEA EFFECT

IKEA is a Swedish home furnishings company known for its modernist design, affordable prices, and innovative retail solutions. IKEA is perhaps best known for putting furniture assembly in the hands of customers.

Instead of selling preassembled pieces, which typically require professional delivery services or special transportation, IKEA packages their unassembled furniture in flat-pack boxes, enabling the customer to transport and assemble it themselves. As IKEA became popular in the United States, naysayers lined up to argue Americans would have little appetite for assembling their own furniture.

This assumption about Americans' disdain for self-assembly proved spectacularly wrong, as the US became IKEA's second biggest market globally.

In 2012, three academics published an article in the *Journal of Consumer Psychology* detailing their research on the valuation of self-made products.[238] The scholars conducted four studies with two sets of consumers. One group, who were amateurs when it came to building furniture, was asked to build IKEA storage boxes. The other group was asked to inspect the same type of IKEA storage boxes that had been assembled by professionals.

Both groups were then given the chance to buy the same object at an auction—one version assembled by a professional and the other self-assembled by the amateur participant in the study. Members of the latter group were willing to pay a 63 percent premium for their own self-assembled IKEA storage box compared to the identical version assembled by a professional.

Why were they willing to pay a higher price for the same item assembled by an amateur and not a professional? These consumers saw the self-assembled item as an extension of themselves, a signifier of their own skill and competence, so they endowed it with greater value. The researchers deemed this phenomenon the "IKEA effect" and described it as "the increase in valuation of self-made products."[239]

Every strategist should remember the IKEA effect when doing strategy work. Yes, you may be technically able to build and execute a new strategy with a small, elite team. But how will you get the rest of your organization to truly buy into the overall process and product?

The IKEA effect illustrates why it's critical to keep widening the circle of authorship in doing strategy work. Better engagement leads to greater value. Greater value feeds more ownership. And more ownership is your best chance of nurturing more strategists.

3 CHOICES

Where to Play
When to Strike
How to Win

WHERE TO PLAY

Do you know the name Roger Federer? Probably so. Do you know the name Lin Dan? Probably not. The former is one of the best tennis players of all time. The latter is considered the greatest badminton player of all time.

Federer has earned $130 million on the court during his playing career. (He's also secured nearly $800 million in endorsements.) Dan has earned $26 million. Both made their living by being the best in the world with a racket. The difference?

The answer is industry disadvantage.[240] Top players in tennis earn ten to twenty times more on the court than top players in every other racket sport.[241] Endorsement deals follow the same logic. In short, no matter how dominant a badminton player becomes, they will never earn as much money as a good—but not great—tennis player.

The lesson to learn? Context matters. For both individuals and organizations, the decision of where to play has a substantial effect on a strategy's success or failure. Strategists know a simple truth: A great strategy is no match for the wrong context.

Based on decades of strategy consulting experience, the authors of *Your Strategy Needs a Strategy: How to Choose and Execute the Right Approach* believe context is the most overlooked and underestimated variable in strategy work.[242] For them, the best organizations start with a thorough assessment of their environment and work backward, matching the right strategy to the right context.

FIVE ENVIRONMENTS FOR STRATEGY

The authors delineate five standard environments for strategy work:

Classical: This environment is predictable but not malleable. Strategies center on leveraging size, scale, or capabilities to gain further advantage in a relatively stable competitive landscape. Traditional planning is common here. Strategic aim: *Be Big.*

Adaptive: This environment is unpredictable and nonmalleable. Strategies center on adapting to constant, fast-paced change by experimenting, innovating, iterating, and prototyping. Given the sheer speed of change, traditional planning is no match for this disruptive climate. Strategic aim: *Be Fast.*

Visionary: This environment is predictable and malleable. Strategies center on being first to market with a breakthrough idea, product, or model. The goal is to shape a new landscape or reshape an existing one. It's less about having a traditional plan and more about building a visionary approach rooted in imagination and innovation. Strategic aim: *Be First.*

Shaping: This environment is unpredictable but malleable. Strategies center on collaborating with others to create a robust ecosystem that can shape or reshape an industry. Planning focuses less on secrecy and competition and more on collaboration, coordination, and scaling. Strategic aim: *Be the Orchestrator.*

Renewal: This environment is unforgiving. Strategies center on doing whatever it takes to survive the next wave of bad results before pivoting to one of the other four archetypes to reset your overall strategy. Planning amounts to a two-phased approach. First, play defense to shore up your standing and build up your viability. Second, shift from defense to offense as soon as possible. Strategic aim: *Be Viable*.

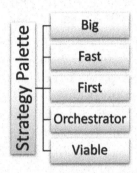

WHERE TO START

Where should you start in discerning the relationship between your environment and your strategy? The authors suggest looking around to spot examples of misalignment. What organizations pursued a classical strategy while operating in an adaptive environment? What organizations tried implementing a visionary strategy when they should have been building an ecosystem with a shaping strategy? What organizations failed to pivot from defense to offense within a renewal strategy?

The authors claim the best organizations see the five-environment model as a strategy palette. Choose the right strategies for the right conditions, pivoting from one archetype to another in a smooth and timely fashion. It's similar to an artist using a multicolor paint palette to bring different scenes to life on the same canvas.

Successful organizations also develop multiple, context-driven strategies for each of their product lines or geographical units, pursuing an adaptive strategy in one area and a shaping strategy in another. Whether it's a sequential or simultaneous deployment of the strategy palette, the key is for your organization to be acutely aware of its context at all times and adapt its strategies accordingly.

If *Your Strategy Needs a Strategy* has a key takeaway, it's this: no strategy lives independent of a context. Where an organization chooses to play is one of the most important decisions to be made when doing strategy work. It's why no strategist can afford to treat context as an afterthought.

What happens when you misread the context? You get Colgate selling frozen meals. Cheetos selling lip balm. Life Savers selling soda. Harley Davidson selling perfume. *Cosmopolitan* selling yogurt. ESPN selling a mobile phone. Bic selling disposable underwear. And Hooters selling seats on its own airline.

In their original context, each of these brands was highly successful. If anything, most of them commanded the top spot in their respective domain. Yet when they applied their strategies to a different context, they failed to the point of ridicule. Again, context matters.

As you reflect on the role of context, don't lose sight of your competitive landscape.

Here another analogy from the tennis world may prove helpful.[243]

In professional tennis, playing defense against your opponent rarely leads to victory because professionals don't make many mistakes. You win the match by making winning shots. In amateur tennis, playing defense against your opponent typically leads to fewer mistakes by you and more by them. You win the match by not making losing shots.

Is your context calling for you to make winning shots or to force losing shots?

Knowing which shot to take is critical to being a strategist. But so is changing the nature of the game as needed. As the strategists David Yoffie and Michael Cusumano illustrate: "Good strategists calculate their competitors' most likely actions and figure out how to counter those moves. A master strategist goes one step further and figures out how to change the nature of the game, typically by altering the other players' options and payoffs."[244]

STUDY YOUR CONTEXT

As a strategist, you must establish a routine for studying your context. Trust your where-to-play choices will only be as sound as your what-to-expect forecast.

One way to build a sustainable routine is to pursue a parallel approach of thinking from the outside in and the inside out.

For your outside-in work, gain as much perspective on the broader world as possible. For instance, finish at least two podcasts a month on macro-level trends related to technology, talent, transportation, demographics, or the like. Read at least two books by a future-focused thinker every year. Identify one deep thinker every month and ask them to share their predictions on where society is headed. Dedicate at least two hours a week to studying issues within your industry but beyond your organization.

Raja Rajamannar, the chief marketing and communications officer at Mastercard, devotes six hours a week to studying developments in and around his industry.[245] His book *Quantum Marketing: Mastering the New Marketing Mindset for Tomorrow's Consumers* is a context-driven approach to strategy in the marketing domain.

Countless other strategists quietly devote considerable amounts of time and attention to studying their context.

You get the point: create a cadence to your learning and keep score.

For your inside-out work, analyze how your organization's environment has evolved. How has your context changed from the past to the present? How do you anticipate your context to change from the present to the future?

Given Jeff Bezos's historic success as a strategist, he's often asked to predict the future. People want him to forecast how the world will change in the next ten years. For him, the more interesting question, rarely asked, speaks to the opposite reality: What's *not* going to change in the next ten years?[246]

As Bezos explains, "And I submit to you that that second question is actually the more important of the two—because you can build a business strategy around the things that are stable in time....[I]n our retail business, we know that customers want low prices, and I know that's going to be true 10 years from now."[247]

He continues, "When you have something that you know is true, even over the long term, you can afford to put a lot of energy into it."[248]

As you study your context, both from the outside in and from the inside out, remember Max McKeown's observation: "Strategists see what others miss."[249]

YOUR WALTON MOMENT

If studying your context seems too boring or burdensome, consider the backstory behind Sam Walton's trip to South America in the 1980s.[250] Walton, the founder and chairman of Walmart, visited friends in Brazil. Assuming he was out sightseeing on his own, his friends were shocked when the police called and asked them to pick up Walton from the local jail.

Walton, already in his sixties and a billionaire many times over, had been arrested at a competitor's retail store. The offense?

The multibillionaire was crawling around on the store's floor, measuring the width of the aisles. Walton, the perpetual strategist, couldn't keep his curiosity in check. He had to learn more about how the context in Brazil might impact his strategy work moving forward.

When it comes to studying your context, what's your Sam Walton-on-the-floor moment?

STRATEGIST'S NOTEBOOK

CHOOSE TO WIN

Tide. Bounty. Dawn. Downy. Crest. Head & Shoulders. Febreze. Charmin. Mr. Clean. Swiffer. Pampers. Old Spice. Secret. Puffs. Pantene. Cascade. Gain. Bounce. Olay. Pepto Bismol.

Good luck finding an American home that doesn't have at least one product made by Procter & Gamble.

A. G. Lafley served as CEO of P&G from 2000 to 2010 (and again from 2013 to 2015). A writer at *Fortune* describes Lafley as "one of the most lauded CEOs in history."[251] In 2013, Lafley teamed up with strategy consultant Roger Martin to coauthor the book *Playing to Win: How Strategy Really Works,* a detailed account of how the two strategists reimagined P&G's enterprise-wide approach to strategy.[252]

WINNING AND CHOICE

Lafley and Martin define strategy as "an integrated set of choices that uniquely positions the firm in its industry so as to create sustainable advantage and superior value relative to the competition."[253] For them, strategy runs on the twin engines of winning and choice. If you aren't deeply committed to both, you don't have a viable strategy.

For Lafley and Martin, strategy boils down to a cascade of five mutually reinforcing choices: 1) winning aspiration, 2) where to play, 3) how to win, 4) core capabilities, and 5) management systems.[254]

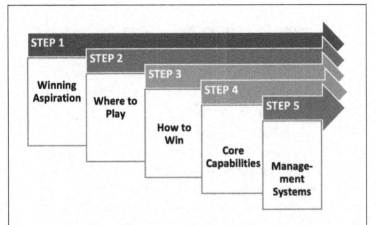

FIVE REINFORCING CHOICES

Winning aspiration: Strategy must start with a clear vision of what success looks like. The more general the description, the more problematic subsequent choices become because it suggests your organization is playing to play instead of playing to win. You must also guard against mediocrity: "A too-modest aspiration is far more dangerous than a too-lofty one. Too many companies eventually die a death of modest aspirations."[255]

A winning aspiration is bold and specific. It stems from your organization's mission, purpose, and talents. It centers your thinking on customers. It takes stock of the competitive landscape. Lastly, a winning aspiration is only as good as the choices and actions behind it.

Where to play: Not even a great strategy can survive the wrong context. Your vision for winning must be grounded in a deep analysis and decisive choice of where to play. Where-to-play choices may involve geography, customer segments, product types, pricing tiers, distribution channels, partnership networks, and so on.

The authors recount the story of Liquid Tide as a where-to-play example.

When P&G launched Liquid Tide, the market was dominated by Wisk. Instead of trying to convince Wisk customers to switch brands, P&G chose to expand the playing field by persuading more consumers to use liquid detergent. Since these new customers to liquid detergent had no allegiance to Wisk, Liquid Tide became their brand of choice. By the time P&G decided to position Liquid Tide to compete head-to-head against Wisk, the former had gained so much momentum that it overtook the latter for the top spot in the overall market.

The reverse is also true: Deciding where not to play is an equally important choice that must inform your strategy.

How to win: "Where-to-play and how-to-win choices do not function independently; a strong where-to-play choice is only valuable if it is supported by a robust and actionable how-to-win choice."[256] There are multiple ways to win in any field of play.

Two common methods are price leadership and differentiation. Think of Walmart for the former and Apple for the latter. You also can create your how-to-win choices based on your organization's unique strengths. "But don't kid yourself either. If, after lots of searching, you can't create a credible how-to-win choice, find a new playing field or get out of the game."[257]

Core capabilities: "An organization's core capabilities are those activities that, when performed at the highest level, enable the organization to bring its where-to-play and how-to-win choices to life."[258] Taking your existing organizational strengths and simply making them better is not a winning strategy. These strengths may not be integrated and optimized or built for tomorrow's competitive landscape.

The aim is to build an ecosystem of fully integrated core capabilities that mutually reinforce one another, leading to a strategy that's "feasible, distinctive, and defensible."[259] Since all capabilities are not created equal, organizations should "invest disproportionately in building the core capabilities that together produce competitive advantage."[260]

Management systems: "But even if you set a winning aspiration, determine where to play and how to win, and define the capabilities required, strategy can still fail—spectacularly—if you fail to establish management systems that support those choices and capabilities."[261] At P&G, the goal was to create strategists at every level.

The authors started by overhauling meetings from a parade of "sell-and-defend" presentations to a series of dialogues on strategic topics identified in advance. The strategic dialogues were underpinned by assertive inquiry, a new cultural norm that "blends the explicit expression of your own thinking (advocacy) with a sincere exploration of the thinking of others (inquiry)."[262]

They also introduced an enterprise-wide framework for planning called the OGSM: "a one-page document that captures objectives, goals, strategy, and measures for a brand, category, or company."[263] Like core capabilities, management systems must drive the success of your where-to-play and how-to-win choices.

ADAPTING P&G'S PLAYBOOK

As a strategist, you can borrow any number of pages from P&G's playbook. Below are six questions to get you started.

1) Does your organization have a winning aspiration?

2) Has your organization determined where not to play?

3) When was the last time your organization made a how-to-win choice?

4) Do your core capabilities and management systems advance your where-to-play and how-to-win choices?

5) What would have to be true for your organization to fully embrace the culture of playing to win and making tough choices?

6) What would have to be true for your organization to train and support more and better strategists at all levels?

Playing to Win remains one of the most popular strategy books of all time. Every strategist should have a working knowledge of its key takeaways.

WHEN TO STRIKE

By anyone's standard, YouTube has been wildly successful. The most popular video-sharing platform in the world welcomes more than two billion users per month. Yet what if YouTube had launched its strategy in 1995 rather than 2005?

The dial-up technology of the 1990s would have made it virtually impossible for YouTube to survive, much less thrive. Timing.

A cofounder of Warby Parker insists the company would not have succeeded had they launched their strategy prior to 2010.[264] In his words, "We had to wait for Amazon, Zappos, and Blue Nile to get people comfortable buying products they typically wouldn't order online."[265] Timing.

Lisa Kahn has studied the financial effects of graduating college in a bad economy.[266] Her initial finding seems obvious enough: Graduates who enter a bad economy have fewer job options and lower wages than graduates who enter a good economy. Her next insight seems less predictable: Fifteen years later, the graduates who landed in a bad economy were still earning 2.5 percent less than graduates who entered a good economy. Timing.

Bill Gross has launched more than one hundred companies via his start-up studio. Seeking to discern why some start-ups succeed while others fail, Gross analyzed the trajectories of two hundred companies over twenty years.[267] He found several factors seeded success, such as a disruptive idea, innovative business model, savvy leader, strong team, and sufficient funding.

But none were more important than when the strategy was launched: "Timing accounted for 42 percent of the difference between success and failure."[268] Timing.

Strategists understand and embrace the power of when. They are students of timing.

In making strategic choices, they know when to strike is equally important as where to play. Strategists study timing at multiple levels—from the individual to the organization to everything in between. Where others assume chance, they look for timing.

INDIVIDUAL TIMING

To understand timing from an individual perspective, Daniel Pink's *When: The Scientific Secrets of Perfect Timing* is a good place to start.[269] Pink unearths the timing habits and biases behind how individuals make decisions.

Did you know Google searches for the term "diet" increase 82 percent at the start of the year, 14 percent at the start of the week, and 10 percent after a federal holiday?[270] Did you know gym visits increase at the start of a week, month, and year?[271] Why?

Since humans have a penchant for fresh starts, these temporal landmarks see more activity because of their symbolic significance.

Did you know forty-nine-year-olds are three times more likely to run a marathon than a fifty-year-old?[272] Did you know twenty-nine-year-olds are two times more likely to run a race than individuals one year younger or older than them?[273] Why?

In the final year of a life decade, people (social scientists call this group the 9-enders) are more preoccupied with the degree of meaning in their lives and thus seek to test it.[274]

In addition to running marathons, 9-enders are more likely, tragically, to commit suicide or to have an extramarital affair.[275] Pink believes the symbolic weight of endings—in this case, the end of a life decade—can lead individuals to act in dramatically different ways.[276]

Beginnings and endings play a subtle but significant role in how individuals make decisions. Yet midpoints matter too.

When it comes to teamwork, research shows groups start with high hopes but rarely get much done out of the gate. Inertia lasts until the temporal midpoint of their work—exactly halfway between the start date and deadline—and then a burst of activity occurs. This heightened focus and tangible progress creates a tailwind that then leads the team to meet the deadline.[277]

As Pink concludes, the temporal midpoint serves as an alarm bell for teams, injecting "a healthy dose of stress—*Uh-oh, we're running out of time!*—that revives our motivation and reshapes our strategy."[278]

As a strategist, Pink teaches you how to spot the power of beginnings, middles, and ends.

ORGANIZATIONAL TIMING

To understand timing from an organizational perspective, Rita McGrath's *Seeing Around Corners: How to Spot Inflection Points in Business Before They Happen* is worth reading.[279]

McGrath, a strategy professor at Columbia Business School, believes organizations are at their best when they spot an inflection point on the horizon and then shape and time their strategy play accordingly.

An inflection point is a 10x change that upends the core assumptions of an organization.[280] The aim is to anticipate the disruption and its timing, not simply react to it.

To spot inflection points, McGrath recommends gathering intelligence from the edges of the organization, engaging directly with the external perspectives, seeking out diverse voices, fostering little bets that facilitate learning about how the world is unfolding, creating incentives for inconvenient information to surface, developing an early view of the future by engaging with futurist thinkers, and studying leading indicators that are more emergent than assembled.[281]

Good and bad examples of organizational timing are everywhere. Two interesting ones to consider are Airbnb (2008) and Uber (2009). The former anticipated an inflection point in lodging, the latter in transportation. Both believed customers wanted better pricing, optionality, and flexibility.

From a timing perspective, both companies were trying to launch against the backdrop of a major recession. Either of them could have postponed their launch until the economy more fully recovered. They instead used timing to their advantage, recruiting hosts (Airbnb) and drivers (Uber) who were hungry to earn in a still-weakened economy.[282]

Both Airbnb and Uber leaned into the timing of the recession and converted a potential obstacle into a breakthrough opportunity.

POWER OF WHEN

As a strategist, you must force your organization to be more aware of and adaptive to the power of timing.

Start by studying the timing of your organization's last strategy. Did it anticipate or react to an inflection point?

What corners did you see around? What corners did you miss? Was the timing of the launch effective? What did the midpoint look like? Was there a definitive ending—and, if so, what did it accomplish? On the whole, was timing a meaningful part of the discussions on how to position your strategy for sustained success?

Think of your next strategy. How will you integrate questions of timing into your thinking and planning? What will you do differently to spot a strategic inflection point before it happens? How could you spark an inflection point on your own? What would it look like to be too early or too late with your strategy?

Don't be preoccupied with being first to market. Google wasn't the first mover to search. Facebook wasn't the first mover to social networking. Apple wasn't the first mover to personal computers or smartphones. Netflix wasn't the first mover to home entertainment. And Home Depot wasn't the first mover to hardware.

What launch date would have the most symbolic significance for your organization? What launch date would disrupt your competitors? How would you leverage the midpoint of your strategy to create that extra boost of motivation and momentum? What is the ideal pace for your strategy? What type of ending for your strategy would elevate your organization to a higher plateau for future strategy work?

Strategists keep Neal Cabage's observation top of mind: "You can afford to get a lot of other things wrong if you get your timing right."[283]

STRATEGIST'S NOTEBOOK

ADJACENT POSSIBLE

Tune In, Hook Up was launched in 2005 as an online dating service. The strategy was a complete failure, but the company's technology for uploading videos in a fast and easy fashion was a breakthrough success on its own. The company was renamed YouTube.

The business model for this 2009 start-up included a fleet of luxury black cars operated by professional drivers with commercial licenses. The strategy shifted to allowing everyday drivers, who passed a background check, to use their personal cars to transport customers at a more competitive price point. The company rebranded from UberCab to Uber.

Burbn was an app designed to help individuals meet up at certain times and locations and then share photos of their experience. In 2010, once the founder realized his platform was heavy on features and light on users, he stripped his strategy down to its best part: a fast and easy photo-sharing site. He renamed it Instagram.

This company started in 1997 as an online rental store that mailed DVDs to customers via the US Postal Service. Their strategy successfully predicted the descent of DVD sales and the rapid rise of streaming video content on demand. You know them as Netflix.

Odeo was designed in 2005 to be a platform for podcasting. But once Apple announced iTunes would include its own podcasting platform, Odeo's founders quickly realized their strategy could not compete. After brainstorming several alternatives, one of their employees suggested a platform that would allow a user to send a brief text message to one phone number that would then be broadcasted out to the user's entire network of friends. He called it Twttr. Both the strategy and the brand evolved to become Twitter.

The strategy for Relentless.com was to sell music, videos, and books online at lower prices than brick-and-mortar competitors. The founder decided to keep the domain address but changed the company's name to Amazon in 1994. Its long-term strategy of pursuing an expansive list of domain and product categories, ranging from consumer goods to technology services, led to the moniker of the Everything Store.

Based on the concept of the tipping point, The Point sought to bring together a critical mass of people online to rally around a good cause or collective goal. By 2008, the platform evolved to focus on leveraging the collective bargaining power of users to save money on various services in certain cities. Their strategy to match interested groups with desirable coupons led to a rebranding of the company to Groupon.

Since the gaming company Tiny Speck had employees working across the country trying to create a new game called Glitch, they needed a virtual collaboration tool to assist with communication and project management. They created their own productivity tool for internal use. Although the company's gaming strategy was slumping, their internal productivity tool proved better than any other one they had seen in the marketplace. The founder decided to scrap Tiny Speck in 2014 and instead focus on selling the tool to other organizations via a new company called Slack.

Founded in 1998, Confinity focused on building security software for handheld devices. Given the lackluster nature of their strategy, the founders shifted their attention to the fast-growing need for a digital wallet for e-consumers. Confinity then merged with online banking company X.com. The founders developed a singular focus on electronic money transfers for e-consumers and changed their company's name to PayPal.

PIVOTING

What do all of these stories have in common?

Each company successfully executed a pivot. A pivot represents a deliberate shift in strategy that ideally unlocks a new or different set of opportunities for your organization. A pivot can take multiple forms.

Sometimes a pivot entails a fundamental change in direction. Twitter's history reflects this type of wholesale strategy change. Other times a pivot involves a subtle but significant upgrade to an existing strategy. Uber's business model evolved in this way.

Another type of pivot occurs when a distinct part of a strategy is parsed out and scaled to become the whole strategy. Both Instagram and Slack reflect this type of pivot. Most pivots center on fixing a failing strategy. But Amazon has an impressive history of pivoting from a place of strength.

The term pivot has fast become a buzzword, extending beyond its early usage in the start-up world. And this reality alone may cause some to label it as a management fad worth avoiding. If you find the concept useful but the debate about its ubiquity useless, it may be worth turning to the notion of the adjacent possible.

ADJACENT POSSIBLE

Steven Johnson popularized this concept of the adjacent possible in *Where Good Ideas Come From*.[284] It's best visualized as a metaphor by which reality is a room.

Most people keep their thinking contained to this single room. Soon enough, that rigidly defined space starts to limit the range of ideas about the future, about what's possible. Because once thinking shrinks, your sense of possibility does too.

Johnson believes the best way to spark creativity and innovation is to find an adjacent door to this room, one that unlocks a new room with a whole new set of possibilities for the present to reinvent itself. What's more, this new room has an adjacent door of its own, leading to more rooms with more adjacent doors.

And as thinking expands, your sense of what's possible multiplies too. That's the adjacent possible.

If the adjacent possible were a tool, its job would be to keep you from getting stuck in the status quo—in a limiting mindset that walls off other possibilities and opportunities from your deliberate consideration. That's more or less the same objective of a pivot: to unlock a new or different strategy that will keep the status quo from limiting or eliminating your prospects.

No matter the frame used—pivot or adjacent possible—the result is the same. Your strategy needs a strategy to keep it from being tamed by the status quo.

For the strategist, there's no need to wait for signs of failure to start thinking about how you might pivot to fix, upgrade, or completely overhaul your strategy.

Some questions to consider regarding the adjacent possible:

What would a meaningful upgrade to your existing strategy look like?

What would be the hidden advantages of pursuing a wholesale change in your strategy?

What part of your strategy could be divided out and scaled to standalone success?

What new partnerships could unlock breakthrough possibilities for your strategy?

When you pursue a pivot, devote significant time and attention to figuring out the best way to frame your story of transition. As Rory McDonald and Robert Bremner observe, companies that fail to effectively manage the story of their pivot can lose the confidence of everyone involved—from employees to customers to investors.[285]

A strategist's job is to persuade all stakeholders to stick around by explaining why the change is necessary and what happens next.[286] You can do this, according to McDonald and Bremner, by concentrating on three steps: 1) focus on the big picture; 2) signal continuity between where you were, where you are, and where you are going; and 3) move quickly with humility.

Another key to effectively framing your story of transition is to realize the power of because.

In 1978, Ellen Langer published the results of an experiment in which she had people request to cut in line to use the copy machine.[287] They used three different requests, worded as follows:

- "Excuse me, I have 5 pages. May I use the xerox machine?"

- "Excuse me, I have 5 pages. May I use the xerox machine, because I have to make copies?"

- "Excuse me, I have 5 pages. May I use the xerox machine, because I'm in a rush?"[288]

What did Langer find? The first scenario achieved a 60 percent compliance rate. For the second and third, the compliance rate reached 93 percent and 94 percent, respectively.

In short, providing others with the reason for the request—the explanation behind the action—prompted them to be far more supportive of and accommodating with the aim.

As a strategist, never forget the power of because.

HOW TO WIN

Beyond questioning where to play and when to strike, strategists must never tire of asking: How's this strategy designed to win? When it comes to explaining the how behind a strategy, most organizations turn to writing a strategic plan.

In the world of strategy, there's nothing more popular than the strategic plan. There's also nothing more problematic.

STRATEGIC PLAN

Despite their dismal record of success, strategic plans prevail.

Part of the reason is historical. Since your organization produced strategic plans in the past, you simply follow the same routine in the present.

Part is sociological. Your organization believes in the value of the planning process, even if the product is suboptimal. (This logic comes from Dwight Eisenhower's saying that plans are useless, but planning is everything.)

And the biggest part is psychological. The idea of having a detailed roadmap that spells out the exact turns to take to arrive at your desired destination is alluring. A prescriptive plan can offer a sense of order, structure, continuity, and sureness. In the face of uncertainty, these assurances are comforting.

But strategists know strategic plans are anything but strategic.

Most strategic plans die of self-inflicted wounds. More suicide than homicide. The reason? Strategic plans are too complex, calcified, and copious.

As a strategist, you must be able to spot the warning signs.

Too complex: Most strategic plans try to be all things to all people. One way to test for this is to ask how much of the plan involves eliminating initiatives, programs, units, or services. The question of subtraction reveals most plans resemble the opposite. They are built entirely on addition.

When a strategic plan is all options and no choices, the only real decision is self-defeating. How thinly can resources be spread over a sweeping range of crowded opportunities to cover all the bases? If your organization deploys a peanut-butter approach to resource allocation, it's hiding behind complexity and memorializing mediocrity.[289]

Too calcified: Most strategic plans try to detail every action that must be taken throughout the life cycle of the vision. This paint-by-numbers approach fails to sufficiently account for the ever-changing environment that shapes strategy work. As the strategist James Allen observes, since strategy is all about turbulence, abandon the notion of perfect anticipation and embrace the idea of fast adaptation.[290]

What's more, if your strategic plan originates from the C-suite, you're more likely to stay the course, even if circumstances point to a pivot. Why? Gary Hamel, founder of the strategy firm Strategos, says it best: The highest levels of an organization are where you "find people with the least diversity of experience, the largest investment in the past, and the greatest reverence for industrial dogma."[291]

Too copious: Most strategic plans read more like a dissertation than an action plan. Typically, there's a section on history and background; another on mission, vision, and values; and another on goals, objectives, and metrics. And then, there is a smorgasbord of sections on the team, the process for building the plan, an assessment of the context and competition, a SWOT analysis, feedback from constituents, the process for implementing the plan, a glossary of terms, and so on.

If your plan is too long and intricate for your team to read, much less remember, how can you reasonably expect them to implement it effectively?

STRATEGIC DIRECTION

If the strategic plan is destined for defeat, what's a better alternative?

The time has come to pivot to a strategic direction. A strategic direction is more like a compass than a map. It points to rather than prescribes. A strategic direction is best described as being, in Amazon's words, stubborn on vision and flexible on details.[292]

The term direction signifies not only choice but also flexibility. For example, by choosing to go north, you've decided not to head south. That's a strategic choice. Yet, in choosing to go north, you aren't claiming there's only one road to get there. That's strategic flexibility.

A strategic direction includes four interrelated parts: vision, forecast, choices, and impact.

Strategic Vision: This profound and pithy statement distills the essence of your strategy.[293] Unlike a mission statement, which is more aspirational, a strategic vision is action-oriented, enabling individuals at every level of your organization "to *act* quickly by giving them explicit guidance to make strategically consistent choices."[294]

Every Walmart employee understands their organization's loyalty to low prices. They can lead, manage, operate, and collaborate effectively based on the clarity of this strategic vision. For Vanguard, it's high-quality, low-fee investment services. For Allbirds, it's comfort and sustainability. For Disney, it's delighting the customer. For BMW, it's creating the ultimate driving machine.

While your organization's tagline may speak to your strategic vision, the two aren't necessarily the same. The former is a marketing maneuver designed to promote. The latter is a strategy play built to win.

Strategic Forecast: A strategic vision is predicated on a strategic forecast, a theory of things to come. Good strategies don't originate from bad forecasts. You can't expect to win the future if you're unable to anticipate its contours.

To see around corners, you must be able to identify and exploit the trends, patterns, continuities, and discontinuities shaping your world. Zoom in for near-term insights. Zoom out for long-term perspectives.

Remember the cardinal rule: Trying to predict the future as a single point in time—X will happen on Y future date—is a fool's errand. Forecasting is about analyzing the probability of multiple futures. Your organization believes the future will look something like this, so it's betting on that.

Write your strategic forecast in pencil, not pen. It should be tested, updated, adjusted, and refined as much as possible.

Strategic Choices: The drumbeat of your direction, your strategic choices determine where to play, when to strike, and how to win. The strategist Richard Rumelt rightly claims choices are made, not found. There's no choice store to shop from. No prepackaged ideas to order. No how-to videos to watch. No shortcuts to take. Your choices must be hand-built from a thorough analysis of your past, present, and future.

At their best, choiceful decisions impose clarity, feed focus, engender alignment, drive performance, and, ultimately, deliver results. If you aren't making decisive choices, you aren't being strategic.

Strategic Impact: Your strategic direction must articulate the "so what?" behind your overall efforts. Your strategic impact vividly describes what will change as a result of your strategy's success. Go deep to explain the impact behind your impact. Done well, your strategic impact section gives every person associated with your organization a reason to believe, to have faith in things not yet seen.

Beyond these four interrelated parts, an effective strategic direction shares three attributes: It's simple. It's nimble. And it's succinct.

SIMPLE

A strategic direction is simple but not simplistic. Simple is hard because it forces you to eliminate not just bad options but good ones too. Only the best ideas, sharply defined and clearly described, should survive in a strategic direction. Everything else is noise.

The strategist A. G. Lafley agrees, "I found that clearer, simpler strategies have the best chance of winning, because they can be best understood and internalized by the organization."[295] Whereas a strategic plan caters to multiple agendas, a strategic direction pledges its allegiance to a single, clear vision and a curated set of actions.

NIMBLE

A strategic direction is nimble. This agility works on two levels.

First, it's critical to adapt to the fast-changing environment that envelops your strategy. Case in point: The strategic choices you made prior to 2020 were calibrated to a pre-pandemic world. It's hard to imagine how all these same bets could remain unchanged in the face of such historic disruption.

Second, it's necessary to guard against the planning fallacy that assumes everything will go according to plan—also known as the EGAP principle.[296] From the outset, presume things won't unfold precisely as predicted. Replace surprise with readiness. Have enough alertness, openness, and flexibility hardwired into your approach to allow for course corrections.

SUCCINCT

If you can't capture your strategic direction on the front and back of a page, you've failed to impose the type of clarity you need. Clear is crisp. Unclear is verbose. Friedrich Nietzsche says it best: "[I]t is my ambition to say in ten sentences what everyone else says in a book."[297]

If your goal is to have others read and remember your strategic direction, brevity is best.

THE OPPOSITE TEST

In building your strategic direction, a good framing tool to use is Roger Martin's opposite test.[298] Take your strategic vision and ask if the opposite choice is stupid. For example, say your strategic vision is to provide great service to your customers. The opposite would read as follows: to provide poor service to your customers. Sounds stupid, right?

As Martin explains, "It is not as though great service is a bad way to win. It is just that stated at that level of generality and abstraction, it is something that any company in the industry will strive for. Hence nobody does the opposite and it is really not a choice."[299]

The same logic applies to other buzzwords such as excellence, transformative, first-class, or top-notch. If you employ such terms, how are you defining them differently than your peers, and why does that lead to a competitive edge?

STRATEGIC PLAN	VS.	STRATEGIC DIRECTION
complex	→	simple
fixed	→	flexible
addition	→	subtraction
verbose	→	succinct
options	→	choices
activities	→	results
roadmap	→	compass

STUBBORN ON VISION

In charting a strategic direction, what does it mean to be stubborn on vision?

Jeff Bezos explains it as a "willingness to be misunderstood for long periods of time."[300] From his perspective, several of Amazon's most innovative products and services—ranging from the Kindle and Echo to free shipping and customer reviews—were originally met with severe skepticism and criticism. Plus, many of them had a long, bumpy runway to profitability. And yet, Amazon never gave up on them despite the noise from naysayers.

As a strategist, it's worth reflecting on Bezos's philosophy. What would a stubborn vision look and feel like for your organization? How long would you and your team be willing to be misunderstood to pursue your vision? Though stubbornness in pursuing a vision can be a powerful tool, at what point does it become the obstacle to success rather than the way?

PLAN VS. DIRECTION

With a strategic plan, strategy operates like a product—made once, used periodically, and assessed rarely. Why? Products are fixed in time.

With a strategic direction, strategy operates like a service—made continuously, used daily, and assessed regularly. Why? Services are fluid over time.

Another way to discern the difference between a plan and a direction is to compare a VCR to streaming. The VCR is a form of technology. Meanwhile, streaming is a function of technology that can operate across multiple devices. Forms can become dated quickly, especially in the realm of technology. Functions, by contrast, have a much longer runway of relevance. Their odds of seeing the future are much better than forms.

A strategic direction turns your strategy into a function, not a form. Better still, it makes strategy an organizational habit, one that gets fed, watered, and pruned every single day, no matter the weather.

Don't wait for inspiration to get started on your strategic direction.

The painter Chuck Close provides a useful analogy between art and strategy: "Inspiration is for amateurs—the rest of us just show up and get to work."[301] Close continues, "And the belief that things will grow out of the activity itself and that you will—through work—bump into other possibilities and kick open other doors that you would never have dreamt of if you were just sitting around looking for a great 'art idea.'"[302]

The same goes for strategists—just show up and get to work. The best strategies are fashioned, not found.

And don't wait for the ideal time to switch from a plan to a direction. Because the best time to ditch your strategic plan was yesterday. The next best time? Right now.

STRATEGIST'S NOTEBOOK

FLYWHEEL EFFECT
Everything flows from the customer.

A great experience attracts more customers. More customers draw more sellers. More sellers offer better selection. Better selection appeals to more customers. A bigger customer base drives growth and scale that yield lower cost structures. Savings from lower costs are passed along to customers via lower prices. Lower prices and a better experience beckon more and more customers.

As this self-reinforcing cycle loops again and again, it generates accelerated momentum.

Can you guess the company behind this description? Yes, it's Amazon.

Jeff Bezos sketched this virtuous cycle on the back of a napkin in 2001. This was his vision for Amazon's flywheel for sustained success. Did it work?

Amazon's market capitalization was $4 billion in 2001. By 2022, the year Bezos stepped down as CEO, that number had reached $1 trillion. Good luck finding a doodle worth more than that.

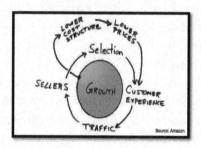

WHAT'S A FLYWHEEL?

A flywheel is a spinning wheel or disc designed to store rotational energy. Historical examples include pottery and water wheels. Modern applications can be found in engines. No matter the setting, the effect is the same: Once set in motion, the rotating power of the flywheel makes it spin with greater efficiency and effectiveness.

The strategist Jim Collins adapted the flywheel concept to an organizational context in his 2001 book *Good to Great*. In 2019, Collins dedicated an entire monograph to the subject entitled *Turning the Flywheel*.[303]

For Collins, a flywheel is an organization's fully integrated and optimized system for sustained success. It's their meta-strategy that shapes every strategic choice.

Each component of the flywheel must be strategically important and dynamic enough to ignite and accelerate momentum in the next component, creating a chain reaction that sustains momentum. Collins calls it "the power of strategic compounding."[304]

HOW TO BUILD A FLYWHEEL

How do you build a flywheel?

Start by generating a list of "significant replicable successes" your organization has achieved.[305] Then compile a list of misses and failures. Compare the two lists to determine which organizational components were integral in the former and lacking in the latter.

Once you've identified the four to six core components that made the difference between success and failure, start developing a rough sketch of your flywheel. Note: If you have more than six components, you need to simplify your list.

Which strategy sets everything else in motion?

That's your starting point. Your next component should flow from there, while the next after that should connect to the previous two, and so on. With a draft sketch in hand, discuss and debate your proposed flywheel, including your choice of components and sequencing, at various levels of your organization.

The most critical feature of any flywheel is the interconnected relationship between the components.[306] Weak, wobbly, misaligned, or friction-laden components are devastating. Why? It not only negatively affects the performance of the next component in the sequence but also compromises the alignment, momentum, and efficacy of the entire flywheel.

To stress-test your flywheel, assign a performance score to each component. Doing so reinforces the reality that low scores tied to underperforming parts can't be tolerated in such an interdependent system. The underperforming components must be improved or replaced because your flywheel will only be as strong as your weakest link.

Large organizations may have multiple sub-flywheels that not only capture the nuance of particular divisions or units but also reinforce the logic, architecture, and efficacy of the primary flywheel.

For Collins, a well-conceived flywheel can drive an organization's strategic success for at least a decade, if not longer, presuming it is renewed and extended. He points to Amazon, Vanguard, and Intel as having savvy flywheels that have been wisely reinvigorated over the years for remarkable staying power.

CONTINUITY AND CHANGE

A flywheel can be a force for both continuity and change at the same time: "On the one hand, you need to stay with a flywheel long enough to get its full compounding effect. On the other hand, to keep the flywheel spinning, you need to continually renew, and improve each and every component."[307] Above all, a sound flywheel keeps your organization relentlessly focused on optimizing the right priorities.

Netflix is another organization that has reaped the benefits of a strong flywheel.[308]

More users create more data. More data feeds smarter algorithms. Smarter algorithms provide better AI-generated recommendations for users. Better recommendations further enhance the user experience. A better user experience attracts even more users. As this self-reinforcing cycle loops again and again, it generates accelerated momentum.

And the results speak for themselves. In 2011, Netflix served 24 million users. By 2022, this number reached 221 million. In 2011, the average user spent 310 hours per year on Netflix. By 2022, this number reached 1,168 hours per year.

FORCING FUNCTION

Injecting strategy into your organization's everyday life can be a chronic challenge, especially early on. Too many organizations relegate strategy discussions to a retreat once or twice a year. Strategists know that cadence simply doesn't work.

You must create the space and conditions for strategy conversations to flourish daily within your organization. And the flywheel concept is a helpful means to this end.

It's nearly impossible to discuss the components of a flywheel, including the sequencing and efficacy of the parts, without finding yourself contemplating issues of strategy. Take another look at Amazon's flywheel, and you can see how strategic choices reside at every turn. You can also imagine how each of their six components has a sub-flywheel of its own.

If your organization seems suspect of the entire endeavor, assuming the flywheel exercise is a management fad destined to be discarded, share this image from the creative mind of Walt Disney. As early as 1957, he was working on his version of the flywheel effect.[309]

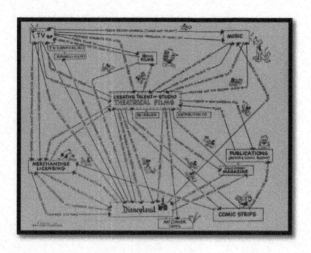

PERSONAL FLYWHEEL

As a strategist, what does your personal flywheel look like? What points are causing friction? What points are accelerating momentum?

2 FIXES

Make Smart Bets
Secularize Strategy

MAKE SMART BETS

Strategy is often defined as making choices. Your strategy compels you to decide yes or no, this or that, here or there, now or then. True, strategy is a decision-driven endeavor. But relying entirely on the language of choice to describe strategy is limiting in two ways:

First, the language of choice understates the risk associated with strategy work.

For instance, an organization can maintain its current aims and ways. That's a choice, one that can be made with a high degree of confidence and comfort. But what if that sureness is precisely the problem?

The strategist Roger Martin believes fear and discomfort play an essential role in strategy work.[310] A good strategist, in Martin's view, should be uncomfortable and apprehensive because they force themselves to stretch beyond the status quo, to work outside their comfort zone in building and launching a risk-based strategy.[311] Choice doesn't adequately convey this risk and doubt.

Second, the language of choice undersells the consequences of strategy work.

Organizations make countless choices every year without ever asking a basic question: Was this a winning or losing strategy in the end?

A good strategy forces you to keep score of the consequences of your decisions. That situational awareness, in turn, keeps you constantly on guard to maintain your lead or dig deeper to close the gap. As Martin explains, "In fact, if you are entirely comfortable with your strategy, there's a strong chance it isn't very good."[312]

Strategists know that framing strategy solely in the language and logic of choice is overly narrow.

A better fix? Define strategy as an exercise in making smart bets.

STRATEGIC BETS

The strategy consultant and retired poker champion Annie Duke defines a bet as "a decision about an uncertain future."[313] Sounds a lot like strategy, right?

Here are five ways strategy work mirrors the world of betting.

❶ *Simple Truth*

Betting is built on a simple truth: you can't win by watching.

To see success, you must be willing and able to place a bet on the table and play the game at hand. No bet means, and necessarily so, no option to win. It's that simple.

The same truth applies to organizations. To create success, your organization must be willing to put a sound strategy into play. Simply watching other organizations play to win rarely carries the day.

Your organization must have the foresight and fortitude to make a bet on how you think the future will unfold. Think of your strategy as the minimum bet required for your organization to have a seat at the table. No bet via strategy means no chance of winning big.

❷ *Clear Stakes*

In betting, the stakes are always clear.

You know exactly how many chips you have on the table and their corresponding value. And everybody else knows it too. There's no guessing as to what's at stake when you look around the table.

Strategy should operate the same way. Everyone around you must possess a clear understanding of your strategy, including its purpose and value, as well as the stakes associated with its success or failure.

❸ *Inescapable Risk*

Betting involves an inescapable level of risk.

If you place a bet, you always have a chance of losing. There's no way to extinguish this risk. It's always already there because every potential reward comes with an unavoidable risk. Yet the downside of a bet is capped. You can't lose more chips than your bet on the table.

Strategy must incorporate risk too. You should have something meaningful on the line in pursuing your strategy, the loss of which would cause your organization to feel the consequence, learn from the situation, and vow to do better next time.

If you can't articulate the sacrifices you have made to launch your strategy, there's a good chance you're not stretching far enough.

To be clear, taking a risk isn't the same as being risky.

The former represents a highly calculated bet on how to use strategy to bend the future in your direction. The latter amounts to impulsively taking a chance on something and simply hoping for the best. Like a bet, strategy is best served when the downside risk is capped.

❹ *Undeniable Luck*

Betting bows to luck.

Duke says it best: "You could teach someone the rules of poker in five minutes, put them at a table with a world champion player, deal a hand (or several), and the novice could beat the champion. That could never happen in chess."[314]

Since poker is a game of incomplete information and uncertain variables, luck always has a seat at the table. Players ignore this reality at their own peril.

The same holds true for strategists.

Luck is always a variable in every strategy. If you know a self-described strategist who underestimates the role of luck in their work, there's a good chance they're the dumb money at the table.

❺ *Knowable Odds*

Betting is built on odds, a measure of the likelihood of winning, losing, or tying.

Professional card players continuously assess their odds of winning throughout a game. Knowing they can't eliminate the inherent risk associated with playing the game, these professionals instead focus on first discerning and then leveraging their best odds of winning.

Martin describes strategy work in much the same way: "Strategy isn't about finding answers. It's about placing bets and shortening odds."[315]

The strategist Sven Smit echoes this sentiment, insisting strategy development is least effective when management teams seek certainty rather than gauge odds.[316] Smit continues, "In business, as in poker, there is uncertainty, and strategy is about how to deal with it. Accordingly, your goal is to give yourself the best possible odds."[317]

POKER VS. SLOTS

Ever wonder why professional gamblers steer clear of slot machines?

It's a game of chance, not skill. And the odds of winning rank among the worst in a casino.

Acutely aware of this reality, professional gamblers migrate to other casino games, because they know they can employ their expertise and experience to increase their odds of winning.

Their strategy is simple yet profound: Don't play a game that offers unskilled amateurs the same odds of winning as skilled professionals. Instead, play a game that allows your strengths—or your competitor's weaknesses—to directly increase your likelihood of winning.

The same logic extends to organizations.

Don't pursue a strategy that gives your competitors the same—or, worse yet, better—odds of winning the future you want. Instead, build a strategy that plays to your organization's strengths and seeks every advantage possible to tilt the odds in your favor.

This question of where to play in gambling—such as poker or slots—is equally important in the world of strategy. Martin Hirt and his colleagues at McKinsey's Strategy Practice tracked the profit margins of the world's largest companies over ten years and found this decision of where to play accounted for roughly 50 percent of the firm's performance.[318]

Hirt explains, "The role of industry in a company's position is so substantial that you'd rather be an average company in a great industry than a great company in an average industry."[319]

As a strategist, one way to train yourself to think in terms of odds—and to calibrate your efforts accordingly—

is to plot your strategy decisions along a spectrum of probability and impact.

For instance, if you encounter a strategy decision that's low in probability and low in impact, how would you respond? Low probability and high impact? High probability and low impact? High probability and high impact?

	Low Probability	High Probability
Low Impact	Bet Small & Be **AWARE**	Bet Moderately & Be **READY**
High Impact	Bet Moderately & Be **SAVVY**	Bet Big & Be **DARING**

This matrix represents an example of how you might structure your thinking and calibrate your focus as you contemplate your strategy decisions.

Notably, your bets should be squarely aligned with your risk appetite, your core capabilities, and, above all, your strategic direction.

And don't forget about luck!

BET BIG & BE DARING

A telling example of a big and daring bet is Google's acquisition of YouTube for $1.65 billion in 2006.

At the time, most experts claimed that the price was too high and that the long-term value was overstated. Nevertheless, Google saw around the corner and concluded it was the right bet at the right time for their far-sighted strategy.

Today, most analysts estimate YouTube's valuation to be in the $160 billion to $300 billion range.[320] Beyond a smart bet, the acquisition proved to be a savvy one.

In 2006, Google's own video platform, Google Videos, struggled to compete. They could have sunk more time, resources, and brand equity into their own platform. That may have seemed like the safer bet at the time.

And yet, Google's leadership believed in their forecast, bet big on their strategy, and tilted the odds of success in their favor. Then they proceeded to crush the competition in short order.

Another telling example is Netflix and its commitment to actively nurture a culture of betting on strategies.

Once or twice a year, the CEO directs managers to complete a form that filters their previous bets into three categories: "bets that went well, bets that didn't go well, and open bets."[321] As the CEO explains, "This exercise reminds everyone that they are expected to implement bold ideas and that, as part of the process, some risks won't pay off."[322]

FIVE STEPS FOR BETTING ON YOUR STRATEGY

Situating your strategy work in the context of betting forces you to think in more concrete and consequential terms.

Here are five steps to make smarter strategy bets:

1) Pick wisely where to play. Think poker (more skills), not slots (more chance).

2) Gauge your odds of winning early and often and adapt accordingly.

3) Put something meaningful on the line.

4) Take risks without being risky. Find the down-hill opportunity.

5) Let the right alignment of probability, impact, and luck guide the size of your bets.

Thinking in bets reminds you that strategy is always a gamble. No strategy is flawless. No strategy is guaranteed. And no strategy stands the test of time.

Think of strategy the way Natalie Goldberg thinks of poetry: "There is no permanent truth you can corner in a poem that will satisfy you forever.... Stay fluid behind those black-and-white words. They are not you. They were a great moment going through you."[323]

Strategists stay fluid behind the black-and-white words of strategy. They carry no illusions of perfection or per-manence. They are open, honest, and always ready to edit themselves and their work.

Strategists are more than the words that pass through them.

They are poets, not poems.

STRATEGIST'S NOTEBOOK

ZOOM IN, ZOOM OUT

Why are most strategic plans three to seven years in scope? If asked, most leaders say it's best not to be too short or too long in one's thinking. Sounds logical, right? In theory, yes. In practice, not so much. Strategic plans pegged to a medium-term time horizon tend to suffer from two ailments: busyness and incrementalism.

BUSYNESS

Since the strategy's end point is three to seven years in the making, your team can allow themselves to think they always have more time to deliver results. They then spend inordinate amounts of time gathering data, building dashboards, benchmarking peers, perfecting processes, writing the plan, promoting the plan, and so on.

Since everyone remains busy, you presume that all is well and that the outcomes will follow...until they don't. What went wrong?

Your team has fallen prey to the illusion of busyness, whereby they equate being busy with being effective. But managing activities isn't the same as producing results. In short, the perceived cushion of having plenty of time can keep your team from remaining fiercely focused on driving near-term results.

INCREMENTALISM

If you presume your external environment will remain more or less the same over the next three to seven years, your attention invariably turns inward.

The strategic planning process then becomes an exercise in imagining how the organization can become a better version of itself. Though this type of inward focus can lead to critical improvements, it leaves the organization ill-equipped to identify and exploit external trends on the horizon.

As a strategist, how do you guard against busyness and incrementalism?

The strategists John Hagel and John Sealy Brown have pioneered a new paradigm for planning.[324] They call it the "zoom in, zoom out" strategy.

To zoom in, concentrate on the next six to twelve months to drive results. To zoom out, set your sights on what the world may look like ten to twenty years from now and pull that long-term future into your present-day planning. The ideal scenario is to pivot back and forth between the two modalities, enabling each to inform the other.

ZOOM IN

Zooming in on the next six to twelve months provides your best chance of escaping the busyness trap of elevating activities over results. But doing so, argues Hagel and Brown, requires you to overcome the tendency to pursue too many ideas and initiatives at once.

Their advice is to identify "the one near-term initiative that would have the greatest ability to strengthen the business's existing core."[325] Equally important is defunding the initiatives that don't align squarely with your "zoom in, zoom out" strategy and reinvesting those resources.[326] If done well, zooming in creates a clear and contagious sense of urgency.

Zooming in is all about curation. Your mantra: Think gallery, not garage.

ZOOM OUT

Zooming out to the next ten to twenty years provides your best chance of being transformational in your thinking. Unlike a medium-term horizon, it's not as easy to imagine the world ten to twenty years from now.

Doing so forces you to be more creative and visionary in your thinking—especially as it relates to external possibilities. Hagel and Brown describe it as cultivating an outside-in perspective as opposed to an inside-out perspective.[327]

What demographic trends will have prevailed twenty years from now? How will technology, transportation, and disease have altered everyday lives? In what ways will consumption have changed? Will society be more or less social? What industries will have merged? How will populations have clustered in new ways? Will you be serving a different type of customer? Will you be making better versions of your current products or completely different ones?

Long-term inquiries of this nature keep you keenly focused on the world beyond your four walls—where disruption lives. The aim is to disrupt your thinking and strategize accordingly before someone, or something, else does it to you. In short, having the foresight to chart your own path, rather than simply copy or react to another's strategy, is a proven way to seed transformational results.

Hagel and Brown offer a word of caution on zooming out: Don't allow these futuristic conversations to be had but not used. The key is for your team to establish a shared view of what your long-term future will likely engender and then start mapping out strategies in this direction.

In the end, the real magic comes in linking up the big-picture perspective from zooming out with the game-changing results from zooming in.

Zooming out is all about imagination. Your mantra: Think frontier, not fortress.

If you adopt this "zoom in, zoom out" strategy— sharpening your focus on the next six to twelve months as well as the next ten to twenty years— what happens to the time in between?

Hagel and Brown insist if you squarely align your zoom-in thinking and your zoom-out thinking, enabling each to inform the other, the midrange results take care of themselves.

SECULARIZE STRATEGY

You've chosen to be a lifelong strategist. You've defeated the strategy trap. And now you want to activate and support strategists all around you—and help your organization do the same.

What's your next move?

Your biggest challenge doubles as your biggest opportunity. Too many organizations limit strategy work to the C-suite. Doing so turns strategy into dogma and executive leaders into high priests.

Fixing this problem for your organization requires an unwavering commitment to secularizing strategy work, moving the focus from the precious few to the empowered many.

Only then will your organization have an army of strategists operating at all levels.

SELECTIVITY & SCARCITY

The high-priest model of strategy work runs on an endless, self-serving loop.

Organizations get divided into two camps: senior leadership and everybody else.

The former group supposedly has the ability to understand the whole enterprise, balancing complex needs in farsighted ways. The latter group, as the logic goes, only thinks in silos and sprints, caring solely about their short-term wants. In this model, the C-suite builds the strategy, and everybody else simply supports it.

If this sounds like the definition of selective, you're spot on.

By confining strategy work to the C-suite, organizations cap the number of strategists in their ranks. Selectivity breeds scarcity. Leaders assume having a limited number of strategists in-house reflects a limited number available in the marketplace. This tortured logic shines through whenever leaders claim they can't find enough strategists to promote internally or hire externally.

In reality, the high-priest model creates the very crisis—a shortage of strategists—it loves to lament. It restricts strategy work to the C-suite based on the foregone conclusion that the rest of the organization can't be strategic. But since the talent base was never given the chance to be strategists in the first place, they end up getting punished for a crime that was never contemplated, much less committed.

For those who believe the high-priest model is effective, ignore the rhetoric and examine the results. A study involving 124 organizations asked the leaders and managers responsible for executing strategy to name their company's top five strategic priorities.[328]

Sounds simple, right? The people managing the strategy should be able to name said strategy with clarity and accuracy.

And yet only 2.5 of 10 respondents could name three of their organization's top five strategic priorities.[329] Worse still, nearly 4 of 10 respondents couldn't even name a *single* strategic priority.[330]

Before anyone blames this lack of strategic alignment on frontline employees who don't have access to the C-suite, consider one of the study's most revealing findings: the sharpest plunge in strategic alignment occurs between the C-suite and their direct reports.[331]

In sum, the high-priest model of strategy work is broken.

SECULARIZE STRATEGY

For organizations to defeat the strategy trap, the high-priest model must be secularized.

What does secularization mean? Simple: Dethrone strategy's elitism.

Nobody holds the keys to the strategy kingdom. Nobody is above having their strategies questioned, tested, or improved. And nobody is the final arbiter of who can or can't be a strategist.

High priests are neither omnipotent nor infallible. They are tools of the strategy trap. Their gospel saves no one but themselves.

Secularizing strategy is a systematic way to break down the barriers that limit strategists from thriving and multiplying. In helping your organization to secularize strategy, keep three things top of mind:

1. Participation isn't transformation,

2. Hoping isn't doing, and

3. Secularizing isn't democratizing.

PARTICIPATION VS. TRANSFORMATION

In opposing strategy's elitist ways, a growing chorus of thought leaders has been calling for a more inclusive approach to strategy work.[332] The book *Open Strategy: Mastering Disruption from Outside the C-Suite* is the most recent example of this push for organizations to do a better job of engaging more people in strategy work.[333]

Such campaigns are laudable for challenging the dogma of the C-suite. They are also insufficient if the aim is anything more than incremental change.

Saying more people should be involved in strategy work isn't the same as saying the world urgently needs more strategists.

The former is a participation goal—it builds a bigger tent for strategy. The latter is a push to reinvent how organizations define, manage, and grow talent—it builds a bigger tent for strategists.

The strategist A. G. Lafley understands this distinction between participation and transformation. After becoming CEO of P&G in 2000, Lafley set out to cultivate "capable strategists" at all levels of the organization.[334]

Lafley and his longtime strategy consultant, Roger Martin, explain their approach this way: "The idea is to build up strategy muscles over time, in different contexts, so that as managers rise in the organization, they are well prepared for the next strategic task."[335]

With success, these maturing strategists were rewarded with more complex challenges: "This practice-makes-perfect approach to learning strategy explains why so many P&G alums go on to become CEOs."[336]

As P&G's top leader, Lafley did more than merely extend strategy conversations to new corners of the company. He deliberately increased the number, reach, value, and impact of capable strategists beyond the C-suite.

In other words, Lafley built a bigger tent for strategists.

HOPING VS. DOING

"I wish I had fewer strategists at my disposal," said no CEO ever.

No organization, if asked, would decline the benefits of having more and better strategists thriving throughout their ranks. Yet few do anything about it.

Most organizations offer no vision for why strategists matter. No training for emerging strategists. No resources for existing strategists. And no effort to challenge nonstrategic behaviors. Why?

These organizations lack any viable strategies for activating and supporting strategists. They simply hope for the best.

You've heard it before: hope isn't a strategy. The saying is snappy but sloppy.

Not having a well-defined strategy is, in fact, a strategy. It's simply a bad one. To cultivate more strategists, organizations must do it in a systematic, meticulous, and motivating way.

Coaching sports is a helpful analogy to cultivating strategists.

Coaching is:

Self-evident—no team wins without a coach.

Constant—every play, every day, every season.

Organized—with systems, structures, routines, and deliverables.

Focused—seeks to bring out the best performance possible.

Demanding—of the coach and the coached, no matter the score.

Resource dependent—no coach is successful without funding and support.

And though coaching styles differ, the end goal is the same—to be better than yesterday.

Similarly, organizations must adopt a coaching mindset when supporting strategists.

They must explain why prioritizing strategists is essential. They must get organized to better serve the needs of strategists at all stages—new, seasoned, and expert. They must invest heavily in training, resources, and rewards. They must demand more of everyone involved.

Organizations must keep score. Are you hiring enough new strategists? Are you nurturing enough homegrown strategists? Are you serving strategists at all levels? Are you delivering on this mission every day—with no exceptions or excuses?

Organizations must also hold their people accountable for advancing this culture of coaching.

Recall Bill Campbell's mantra: You can't be a great leader without also being a great coach.[337] The same holds true for strategists: You can't be a great strategist without also being a great coach.

If every strategist embraces their obligation to recruit and coach other strategists, and these individuals do the same, the multiplier effect is a game changer for any organization.

Lastly, secularizing strategy shouldn't take years to achieve. Make the case for your organization to host a pitch competition thirty days from now. The aim is to propose strategies on how your organization can grow more and better strategists at every level. Anybody at any level can pitch. Make the stakes matter.

What does your organization have to lose?

Good ideas may lead to upgrades in current strategies or seeds for new ones. Bad ideas reveal how much work is needed to prioritize strategists. Either way, the exercise alone sends a clear signal to the entire organization: Your intent to prioritize strategists is real and getting more robust.

SECULARIZING VS. DEMOCRATIZING

Secularizing strategy doesn't equate to democratizing strategy.

Especially if democratization means every person in the organization gets a vote on which strategy to pursue. And then the leading vote-getter wins the day.

Strategy isn't an election. Nor is it a popularity contest.

Having multiple strategists contribute to a strategy doesn't require having multiple deciders of the final direction. Strategy must be, above all, strategic.

Secularizing strategy is about one thing: making more strategists.

THE COST OF HUBRIS

Organizations that fail to secularize strategy invite, if not compel, their untapped strategists to look elsewhere for opportunities and support. Just ask Disney.[338]

In the 1980s, a young animator pleaded with Disney's leadership to make the budding field of computer animation a strategic priority. Disney declined this strategy recommendation before firing the employee soon thereafter.

The young animator, John Lasseter, then joined Lucasfilm and proceeded to build its computer graphics group into the company now known as Pixar. By the 2000s, Pixar defined and dominated the field of computer animation with mega-hits such as *Toy Story*, *Monsters Inc.*, and *Finding Nemo*.

What company did Disney purchase in 2006 for $7.4 billion? Pixar. Who was named chief creative officer of Pixar and Disney's animation studio at that time? John Lasseter.

The lesson?

Disney already had a visionary strategist on its payroll. Yet Lasseter wasn't sitting in the C-suite. Nor did he have strategy in his title. But he had a theory of things to come. He could see around corners. And his talents were as bold as his desired bets.

All Lasseter needed from Disney was the recognition, resources, and support to be an even better strategist. All he got was disregarded and shown the door.

On the surface, Disney purchased a competitor for $7.4 billion.

But look deeper, and a critical lesson comes into focus: This multi-billion-dollar purchase represents the cost of Disney's hubris, as they had to buy back their previously mismanaged strategist and his game-changing strategies.

How much is it costing your organization to mismanage strategists?

THE WRONG ALTAR

Having dominated strategy's history for so long, the high-priest model has no intention of giving up or giving in. And the strategy trap wants it no other way. It needs to keep preaching the benefits of the high-priest model to maintain its power and privilege.

Even sound thinkers fall prey to this elitist gospel.

In the history of strategy, two books shine the brightest light yet on strategists: Cynthia Montgomery's *The Strategist: Be the Leader Your Business Needs* and Richard Rumelt's *The Crux: How Leaders Become Strategists.*[339] Both authors, publishing more than a decade apart, deserve immense credit for shifting the conversation to strategists.

But even Montgomery and Rumelt find themselves worshipping at the wrong altar. Montgomery focuses on the CEO as strategist. Rumelt limits strategy creation to "a small group of executives" that numbers no more than ten.

Both authors champion strategists while leaving the high-priest model of strategy work wholly intact.

Never underestimate the power and privilege of the high-priest model.

ORGANIZATIONAL SIGNS

How do you know if your organization is on the right track to secularizing strategy?

Here are three promising signs:

- ✓ The C-suite takes concrete steps to prioritize strategists at every level.

- ✓ Strategists thrive because of organizational support, not despite it.

- ✓ Strategists are multiplying in meaningful ways.

STRATEGIST'S NOTEBOOK

SIX STEPS FOR CHANGE

Whether leading, following, or developing the game plan for others to lead and follow, every strategist needs a clear strategy for managing change. Here's a concise six-step strategy for conceptualizing change management:

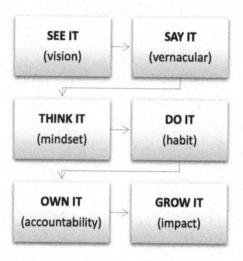

SEE IT

The *vision* stage. You want your people to see and understand the essence of where you must go and why it matters. Imagery and analogies are helpful. Keep the details flexible. Persuade at the level of principle.

SAY IT

The *vernacular* stage. If you want your people to think and act differently, you must give them a new language to do so. Selling a new vision with old language is like trying to bite your own teeth: It is neither effective nor advisable.

THINK IT

The *mindset* stage. You want your people to fully understand who you're asking them to be and what you want them to do. Work from the inside out—from identity to outcomes to change. Persuade at the level of practice.

DO IT

The *habit* stage. You want your people to work on projects that make a meaningful difference in advancing your vision for change. Don't mistake activities for results or movement for progress. Find creative ways to make good habits stick.

OWN IT

The *accountability* stage. You don't want your people merely going through the motions, renting the right words at the right time. You want them to own every outcome. You want them to feel a personal responsibility to deliver their best efforts and sacrifices in service of your desired change.

GROW IT

The *impact* stage. You want your people to feel empowered to grow your strategy in bigger, bolder ways. Provide them with the autonomy, support, resources, and guidance to elevate your original vision to even greater heights.

1 MISSION

Solve for Strategists

SOLVE FOR STRATEGISTS

"Don't be 'a writer' but instead be *writing*."[340] That was William Faulkner's advice to aspiring writers at Princeton University in 1958.

With a Nobel and Pulitzer already to his name, the literary icon knew writers could unwittingly spend more time playing the part of a writer than doing the job of writing. What suffers, ironically, is the writing—the writer's reason for being above all else.

Faulkner's cure is deceptively simple: always be writing.

It's wise counsel for strategists too. Since the discourse on strategists is so underdeveloped, it's tempting to spend your days righting this wrong. But if talking more about strategists results in doing less for strategists, the problem only compounds.

Strategists are walking verbs. They act on ideas. They build the right habits. They break the wrong habits. They defeat the strategy trap. They recruit more strategists. They coach to produce better strategists. And they own every outcome.

So, yes, be a strategist. But be a strategist who's always strategizing.

The best way to always be strategizing is to envision every situation as an equation. Your mission is simple: solve for strategists.

People problem? Solve for strategists.

Process problem? Solve for strategists.

Purpose problem? Solve for strategists.

New opportunity? Solve for strategists.
Growing threat? Solve for strategists.

If you are unsure how to get started, borrow a page from Amazon's playbook.

Among its core leadership principles, Amazon places customer obsession at the top. They capture their strategic intent in three lines: "Leaders start with the customer and work backwards. They work vigorously to earn and keep customer trust. Although leaders pay attention to competitors, they obsess over customers."[341]

You can't work at Amazon and be unaware of or indifferent to their commitment to the customer.

What if you replace "customer" with "strategist" and pursue this obsession with the same zeal? What if you always start with the strategist and work backward? What if you work relentlessly to earn and keep the trust of your strategists? What if you obsess over strategists in every way imaginable?

Once you set your sights on solving for strategists, several challenges start to fix themselves.

OFF VS. ON

Changing CEOs? Most organizations wait until the new leader is ready before launching a strategy build. Hiring a chief strategy officer? Most organizations put their existing strategy on hold until the new expert takes the reins. Closing out the current strategy? Most organizations regroup before starting the strategy process anew. Depending on the situation, these strategy outages may range from weeks to months to longer.

Though the scenarios differ, the effect is the same. Each organization has allowed itself to be driven by circumstance. Strategy has been relegated to a secondary role. Skeptical?

How many organizations can you name that suspend sales, shipping, accounting, or payroll during similar transitions? Spoiler alert: if a function is deemed essential, it never shuts down.

Once you solve for strategists, strategy outages are no longer a threat.

No matter the chaos, your organization never lacks its primary asset: strategists. Strategists keep being strategists despite the inevitable starts, stops, pauses, detours, or gaps within your organization. Their habits, skills, choices, fixes, and mission never stop working for you and your organization.

Strategists give discipline and direction to your organization even, and especially, during times of transition—when the horizon is hard to see. Strategists don't need a formal plan, stated permission, or ideal conditions to be themselves. Nor do they need to be told to keep strategizing on your organization's behalf.

Strategists are self-motivated and self-sufficient.

Strategy is not what they do; strategy is who they are. Since there's no off switch to their identity, there's no interruption to their impact.

Strategists are always on.

CULTURE VS. STRATEGY

Most people know the saying (misattributed to Peter Drucker) that culture eats strategy for breakfast.[342] Culture is shorthand for people. And strategy is synonymous with a plan. The implication is your people are more important than your plan—and don't forget it.

This quote is defined by difference. Culture means one thing; strategy is something else. They aren't the same, nor are they of equal value. Culture not only comes first but also carries the most weight, and the balance is not even close.

Here again, the message is clear: strategy is secondary.

Once you solve for strategists, the logic of this quote implodes. Why? Strategists are your people and strategists are your plan. Both culture and strategy are extensions of the strategist. Once you center on strategists, there's no contrast, no rivalry, and no debate.

STRATEGY VS. EXECUTION

Barrels of ink have been spilled on authors debating the hierarchy between strategy and execution. Is strategy more important than execution? Is execution more important than strategy? Who in the organization is responsible for which realm?

For the strategist Roger Martin, this chronic debate is rooted in a misguided metaphor of the chooser (strategy) versus the doer (execution).[343]

With this trope, senior leaders control the choosing of the strategy, and they expect everybody else to manage the doing of the strategy. But if both groups are in the business of making choices to advance the vision, calling some decisions "strategy" and others "execution" is a pointless distinction, notes Martin. [344]

Once you solve for strategists, the genius of Martin's observation shines through. Choosers must also be doers. And doers must also be choosers. Why?

Both groups are strategists. And strategists must own the entire lifecycle of strategy work—from ideation to implementation and everything in between.

You can't be a strategist and only care about part of the overall equation.

RENT VS. OWN

When strategies fail, as Chapter 2 explains, most autopsies point to the same root cause behind the collapse: a lack of ownership throughout the organization.

This result tends to shock senior leaders, given how much time and resources were spent on seeding the strategy's success.

Consultants were hired. Environmental assessments were completed. An elaborate plan was produced. An implementation schedule was developed. Scorecards, dashboards, and messaging tracks were established. And meeting after meeting was devoted to building, launching, managing, and resourcing the strategy.

In addition to the initial shock of failure, there's an aftershock of disbelief. How could this have happened when the organization was supportive?

Nobody in leadership objected to the strategy. Nobody in management championed a different strategy. And nobody on the front lines said it was asinine. If anything, most people acted as if the strategy made good sense.

What really happened? Your employees played the go-along-to-get-along game.

They said the right words. They took the right steps. And they even gave the right assurances. At no time could they be accused of being anything but supportive of your strategy.

But supporting is not owning.

Supporting is a posture. You provide enough support to avoid blame when the strategy fails. You play the game to play. Owning, by contrast, is a purpose. You do whatever it takes to ensure the strategy succeeds. You play the game to win.

It's the difference between renting strategy and owning strategy.

R E N T	VS.	O W N
me-before-we	→	we-before-me
time teller	→	clock builder
camps downstream	→	pushes upstream
focuses on proving	→	focuses on improving
may-do attitude	→	will-do attitude
sees ahead	→	sees beyond
finite minded	→	infinite minded
mercenaries	→	missionaries

Renting strategy runs rampant among non-strategists. Why?

They see strategy as their organization's want, not as their individualized need. Your strategy has nothing valuable to do with their being—their identity, their growth, their development. When strategy is impersonal, the approach becomes clinical.

And renting is less demanding than owning for them.

Once you solve for strategists, owning strategy is inevitable. Strategists see strategy as an extension of who they are and why they matter. Strategy is air, water, and fire for them. Strategists need it to survive and thrive—to live their identity into action.

Since strategists are always strategizing, renting is not an option.

If a strategy is good, they make it even better. If a strategy is bad, they fix it. Either way, there's zero doubt they own every aspect of it.

HOME VS. OFFICE

The pandemic uncorked a free-flowing debate about remote work.

Many employees can't stop talking about the pros of remote work. Many leaders remain fixated on the cons. Researchers study the impact of remote work on everything from productivity to mental health to commuter costs. And plenty of pundits, podcasters, and consultants treat the debate on remote work as paydirt.

As the conversation continues, one thing is clear: The focus on remote work is far from over. It's easy to see how this topic will dominate future-of-work discussions for many years to come.

But notice what theme is missing from this explosion of research, reports, and reflections on remote work? Yes, you guessed it: strategy.

Where's the robust discussion on whether remote work helps or hurts strategy work?

If strategy suffers during this shift to remote work, it won't be hard to guess why.

Since non-strategists fail to own strategy at the office, it makes sense that working from home produces similar results. If anything, there's a good chance renting strategy has become even more entrenched during this period.

If strategy improved during this shift to remote work, it begs the question of whether remote work vaccinates strategy from the institutional antibodies that plague the office. Can working from home function as an effective edge space, like those detailed in Chapter 10?

Either way, this debate on the pros and cons of remote work would be a nonstarter if organizations had prioritized strategists before the pandemic.

This debate on home versus office is predicated on location.

But the *where* is simply a pretext for the *who*. Isn't the deeper issue at play the camouflaged reality that too many organizations don't trust their employees to be effective at home? After all, institutions tightly control the *where* when they don't trust the *who*.

Prisons, psychiatric wards, and zoos are only the most obvious examples.

Trying to regulate a *who* with a *where* makes no sense in the world of strategists. Where a strategist sits has no bearing on who they are, how they work, and why they matter. Strategists are strategists, always and everywhere.

Once you solve for strategists, you see the massive opportunity organizations missed by not entering the pandemic with an army of strategists already in place. At the very least, they could have sidestepped this whole debate on home versus office.

INCLUSIVE VS. EXCLUSIVE

Consider the main players in the current strategy game—the CEOs, CSOs, strategy consultants, and strategy professors. These are different roles that disproportionately skew to the same demographic profile: white, male, and economically advantaged.

Waiting for these groups to diversify themselves and then to sufficiently diversify the field of strategy seems naive at best. Strategy's history and performance speak for themselves: inclusion is tolerated, not cultivated.

Once you solve for strategists, inclusion is not only unlocked but also unleashed.

Activating more diverse and inclusion-driven strategists dramatically increases the odds of generating more diverse and inclusion-driven strategies.

KILLER VS. KILLED

Every organization wants to own that killer strategy, the one that keeps them winning year after year by a wide margin. But what happens if your greatest asset becomes your biggest liability?

In *The Icarus Paradox: How Exceptional Companies Bring About Their Own Downfall*, Danny Miller identifies dozens of companies that allowed their success to be taken to the extreme, leading to unhealthy levels of certainty, complacency, rigidity, and righteousness.[345]

These once-great companies failed to see how their strategies for victory, over-leveraged and under-scrutinized, created the very conditions for their defeat.

How could highly successful organizations be so blind?

It's the reliable result of being led by strategy, not strategists. Strategy is single-minded. It wants to win. It marches down this path with tunnel vision.

Strategists, by contrast, lead with peripheral vision. Strategists anticipate the need for a course correction. Strategists sniff out when to sunset a winning strategy. Strategists foresee how a win leads to a loss. Strategists know how to avoid the Icarus paradox.

SOLVE FOR STRATEGISTS

Remember every opportunity is an equation. Your mission: Solve for strategists. Your mantra: Make more strategists, make better strategists.

STRATEGIST'S NOTEBOOK

FORCING FUNCTION

During the Qin dynasty in 207 BC, a general named Xiang Yu led an army of twenty thousand soldiers in the Battle of Julu against three hundred thousand Qin forces. After his soldiers crossed the Yellow River, Yu ordered their boats to be sunk and their extra rations to be destroyed.

Yu's army had three days to defeat their enemy or die trying. Despite overwhelming odds against an enemy fifteen times their size, Yu's soldiers prevailed, and he became the king of Western Chu, a territory covering central and eastern China.

Other military leaders throughout history, including the Spanish conquistador Hernán Cortés, took similar measures to eliminate the option of retreat. The phrases "burn the boats," "sink the ships," and "cross the Rubicon" come from this frame of reference.

These point-of-no-return stories illustrate the notion of a forcing function.

By destroying the only means of retreat, these military leaders deliberately force their soldiers to make an either-or choice: win or die. No other option is available.

A forcing function uses constraints to decrease optionality and increase the probability of a preferred behavior or result. Less extreme examples of forcing functions can be found in everyday life:

- IKEA forces shoppers to follow a predefined pathway through every store.

- Twitter forces users to communicate in 280 characters or less.

- UPS forces drivers to decrease left turns and increase right turns.

- eBay forces customers to decide on a purchase within a certain time frame.

- Airlines force pilots to complete a preflight checklist before departure.

On the personal side, paying a personal trainer to come to your house forces you to exercise. Setting a wedding date forces you to decide if marriage is the right choice. Writing in a remote cabin forces you to detox from your digital distractions.

Strategists are no strangers to forcing functions. They constantly look for new or different ways to use forcing functions to drive strategic action.

Consider the five habits outlined in this book. Each is a forcing function:

- Leading time forces you not to waste time.

- Imposing clarity forces you to fight for simplicity and succinctness.

- Thinking in questions forces you to move beyond convenient answers.

- Pushing upstream forces you to focus on sources, not symptoms.

- Seeing around corners forces you to anticipate change, not simply react to it.

Many of the tools spotlighted in this book operate as forcing functions, too. The deep-work day. The #MonkeyFirst exercise. Brainstorming in questions. The six-page memo. Colin Powell's four-step rule for filtering information. The Why Not exercise. Coastguard mode. The future press release. The opposite test. And the list goes on.

As a strategist, you must always be scanning your environment to detect why, where, and how forcing functions are being used or abused.

> What forcing functions are working well within your organization?
>
> What ones need to be reengineered or removed?
>
> How do other organizations leverage forcing functions to their advantage?
>
> How do you use forcing functions to reinforce good habits and eliminate bad ones?

Forcing functions use constraints to shape behavior. And it's easy to assume any restraint hinders your ability to be creative or innovative—to think outside the box.

But Drew Boyd and Jacob Goldenberg disagree.[346] They believe imposing constraints on your thinking actually improves creativity and innovation. Their Systematic Inventive Thinking (SIT) method imposes five types of constraints (subtraction, division, multiplication, task unification, and attribute dependency), each of which forces you to think about your immediate surroundings in new or different ways.

Their mantra is intentionally designed to be iconoclastic: think inside the box to see the familiar in unfamiliar ways.

Take Uber, Airbnb, Alibaba, and Travelocity as telling examples. What do these breakthrough organizations have in common? Each disrupted their respective industry by seeing familiar business models in unfamiliar ways.

All of them subtracted out the primary asset of their respective business model from the standard equation. Uber has no vehicles. Airbnb owns no real estate. Alibaba has no inventory. Travelocity lacks travel agents. Each organization forced itself to think inside the box to see the familiar in unfamiliar ways.

Now apply forcing functions to your organization and its approach to strategists:

How can you force the prioritization of strategists?

How can you force more training and better support for strategists?

How can you force a hiring preference for strategists?

Better still, how can you force the status quo to stop reproducing non-strategists?

O DOUBT

Strategists First

STRATEGISTS FIRST

In pursuing the way of the strategist, be sure to have zero doubt about three things:

1. You can be a lifelong strategist.

2. Your organization needs more and better strategists.

3. The future is defined by a clear-cut choice between strategy and strategists.

FIRST ZERO DOUBT

Have zero doubt you can be a lifelong strategist.

The world wants you to believe you're a strategist only on its terms—if your organization grants you the title, if your boss gives you permission, if you earn that special degree, or if you author that strategic plan. Don't fall for the trap.

Others may govern your where, your when, or your how. But nobody dictates your who.

Your identity is yours—and yours alone. You don't need external validation to be you. You're a strategist as long as you live this identity into action. It's that simple. Don't allow yourself or others to undermine this foundational clarity.

The key is to never rent your identity.

Don't claim to be a strategist only when it's convenient for you or acceptable to them. Being a strategist is never a part-time gig. You must own your identity, always and in all ways. The better the strategist, the more extreme the ownership.

Those who study habit formation know the odds of success increase dramatically when the inputs are improved. Start with the ideal inputs, and the right outputs tend to follow. For you, make your identity your lead input—be deliberate, be disciplined, be daring—and trust the outputs will take care of themselves.

And don't panic if you fall short from time to time.

Remember the analogy of hardcore runners. They have more bad runs or missed runs than they care to admit. It can leave them feeling guilty, frustrated, or dejected. But it doesn't last, because they do whatever it takes to get back to running. Why? Running isn't what they do; running is who they are. They do it to be true to themselves, to their identity.

The same for strategists. You will have more nonstrategic days than you care to admit. And you will have plenty of strategic days that end in subpar results—a faulty forecast, a muddled message, or a bad bet. But don't let a poor outcome undermine a rich process.

Get back to your cadence: five habits, four skills, three questions, two fixes, one mission, and zero doubt. Strategy isn't what you do. Strategy is who you are.

Being true to your identity keeps you grounded, motivated, and determined. Always be you, and always be strategizing.

Since choosing to be a strategist is a life-altering decision, some may want to wait for the right time, the right title, the right boss, or the right backing to take the leap. Waiting for the ideal conditions will only delay your start. As Paul Polman, the former CEO of Unilever, observes: "After all, the only impossible journey is the one you never begin."[347]

SECOND ZERO DOUBT

Have zero doubt your organization needs more and better strategists.

Organizations may not explicitly say they need strategists, but they invariably say they need what strategists bring to the table. Deeper focus. Greater clarity. Savvy forecasting. Better questions. Smarter decision-making. Sticky messages. Clever timing. Add to this list the burning desire for better strategies.

Organizations that have appointed a chief strategy officer (CSO) or the equivalent—and a majority of Fortune 500 firms have done so—are right in theory but wrong in practice. They are right to think they need better help to improve their strategy game. But they are wrong in how they define the CSO's role and responsibility to get there.

First, they treat the strategist as a singular role.

They position the CSO as the general in charge of commanding every aspect of the organization's strategy. Yet they fail to ask the obvious question: Where's the army of strategists trained to fight alongside them?

What battle was ever won with one general and no fighters? No CSO can be effective if they function as an army of one trying to convince non-strategists to fight for strategy.

Second, they give the CSO the wrong focus.

Tasking the CSO to organize, develop, lead, and optimize strategy across the enterprise rarely meets expectations, much less exceeds them. A few years ago, PwC surveyed a cross section of CSOs and found some alarming trends.[348]

- Only 25 percent of CSOs felt "very successful" at creating value for their organization.

- A full 65 percent of CSOs claimed to lack clarity about their role, responsibilities, and priorities.

The best way for organizations to remove such doubt is to give their CSOs a clear and compelling focus: solve for strategists.

The CSO's reason for being is to put strategists first, to build an army of strategists at every level of the organization, to recruit the army, to retain the army, to resource the army, to coach the army, to support the army, to grow the army, and to trust the army.

All strategy then flows from there.

If your organization wants to elevate its strategy game to the next level, dumping more resources into the strategy bucket—without activating an army of strategists—is a race to the bottom between foolish and futile. Max De Pree, the former CEO of Herman Miller, said it best: "In the end it is important to remember that we cannot become what we need to be by remaining what we are."[349]

The best way for your organization to transform its strategy work is to invest in more and better strategists. Full stop.

THIRD ZERO DOUBT

Have zero doubt the future is defined by a clear-cut choice between strategy or strategists.

Dig beneath several macro-level trends within modern society, and you will spot a black swan. The nature of change is changing. Speed is getting faster. Scale is getting smarter. Technology is getting more ambitious. And disruption is getting, well, more disruptive.

The strategist Ram Charan confirms as much: "...the immense uncertainty I see today's business leaders facing is something truly unique. In its scale, its speed, the ferocity of its impact, and its increasing ubiquity, it is qualitatively different—by orders of magnitude—from anything that has gone before."[350]

Other changes are more exaggerated too.

Information is more abundant. Misinformation is more effective. Attention is more divided. Identity is more ambiguous. Institutions are more fragile. Politics is more polarized. Culture is more politicized. Prosperity is more concentrated. Governing is more challenging. Leading is more demanding. And life is more complicated.

The unrest associated with these societal trends shows no sign of lessening, much less reversing. If anything, these markers of volatility seem to be intensifying and mutating.

Though the future has never been simple or sure, its complexity seems more complex.

Charan defines this inflection point as structural uncertainty: "It is structural because the forces now at work can explode the existing structure of your market space or your industry, putting it at risk of being drastically diminished or completely eliminated."[351]

And this structural uncertainty was there even before COVID-19 came and stacked multiple layers of existential threats onto an already hefty load. Will you survive? Your family? Your industry? Your company? Your job?

Prior to the pandemic, you encountered one of these soul-searching questions every few years. During the pandemic, a week rarely passed without being reminded of them all.

The result of this fast, furious, and ferocious change?

Society seems more uneasy about the future, more uncertain about uncertainty.

If the world is more uncertain about uncertainty, where does it turn for help? Strategy seems like the obvious, if not the only, answer.

But take a deeper look at strategy's record, not its rhetoric.

For the past fifty years, strategy has been the dominant paradigm for dealing with uncertainty. Yet take a step back and ask the farsighted question: How has strategy evolved and improved to keep pace with these uncommon times?

Strategy still pledges its allegiance to the strategic plan.

Strategy still operates like an elite country club sport.

Strategy still has a stubborn habit of overpromising and underdelivering.

Strategy still seems self-satisfied, hyping its popularity while downplaying its efficacy.

Strategy still ignores the strategist.

The conclusion is clear: Today's version of strategy looks painfully similar to yesterday's version of strategy. Strategy is petrified.

Strategy's history and performance beg the question: Is strategy the best paradigm to choose when dealing with the unprecedented complexity and uncertainty that lie ahead?

THE BET

How individuals and organizations answer this question means everything.

Those who bet on strategy to win the future presumably do so with one of two theories in mind. They believe strategy is successful now and will be the same moving forward. That's a continuity bet.

Or they believe strategy has the awareness and ability to become successful in the future. That's an improvement bet.

Either bet on strategy is ill-conceived.

First, if the nature of change is changing, betting on a continuity play is risky. Past success rarely guarantees future success in a fast-changing environment. Just ask

Kodak, Blackberry, Blockbuster, or Borders. To win the future, strategy would need to find the will and the way to disrupt itself. That seems implausible.

Second, if strategy can't stop breathing its own exhaust, betting on an improvement play is nonsensical. To win the future, strategy would need the awareness and humility to demote itself, moving from rockstar to roadie. That seems impossible.

Sure, picking strategy for the tricky road ahead could be the right call. Any bet, technically, has a chance at success. But the odds, in this case, suggest otherwise—that picking strategy is reserved for the dumb money at the table.

The smarter choice? Bet on strategists.

Strategists elevate the essential.

Strategists create clarity.

Strategists unlock breakthrough questions.

Strategists fix problems at the source.

Strategists see around corners, anticipating more and reacting less.

Strategists decide where to play and when to strike.

Strategists know how to win with a savvy strategic direction.

Strategists build an army of like-minded zealots at every level.

Strategists ensure strategies are owned, not rented.

Strategists force strategy to evolve in new and different ways.

Strategists stay humble and hungry every step of the way.

If the world is particularly complex and volatile right now, imagine what several years of unparalleled speed, scale, and uncertainty are likely to bring.

Again, the choice to win the future is clear: strategy or strategists?

Smart individuals and organizations understand the choice and clarify the stakes. If strategy fails a majority of the time in today's world, how can it possibly be the wise bet to win a decidedly more complex and uncertain future?

The savvy forecasters will go big on a single bet: The age of the strategist is here to stay.

STRATEGISTS FIRST

Whatever comes your way—doubt, distraction, disruption—just remember to order things by design, not by default.

Strategists first.

Strategists first.

Strategists first.

STRATEGIST'S NOTEBOOK

CRISIS CONVERTED

In a crisis, varying levels of chaos, confusion, and conflict fog the scene. Information is partial. Communication is strained. Relationships are taxed. Time is warped. Clarity is hidden. Focus is fractured. The stakes are high. And fear is real.

In the face of such uncertainty, instability, and risk, organizations have a choice to make: assume bunker mode or activate coastguard mode.

BUNKER VS. COASTGUARD

In bunker mode, the decision is to shelter in place. The organization hunkers down and waits for the storm to pass, hoping the damage won't be catastrophic. Here the goal is to avert disaster. It's a survival tactic rooted in a reactive mindset.

In coastguard mode, the decision is to maintain motion. The organization navigates through the choppy waters of uncertainty to create new openings and options. Here the aim is to convert a crisis into a breakthrough opportunity. It's a deliberate strategy grounded in a resilient mindset.

The biggest difference between bunker mode and coastguard mode? Strategists.

Strategists are never absent a strategy, especially in a crisis. They don't retreat and react. They pursue and attack. They insist on making decisions before decisions make them.

Strategists activate coastguard mode with three steps: point, predict, and pounce.

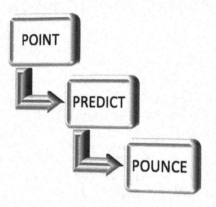

POINT

Early in a crisis, you must point the way forward, beyond the maelstrom of the moment. This means keeping your organization free from succumbing to the unvirtuous cycle of uncertainty, anxiety, fear, and inaction. This loop of helplessness makes it impossible for any organization to face outward and drive forward, to pursue coastguard mode.

The best way to combat this unvirtuous cycle is to bring clarity, structure, focus, and, above all, direction to the table. Enter the point-to-point strategy.

As soon as possible in a crisis, pick an end point to achieve a simple, clear, and concrete outcome. Make the time frame attainable—such as the end of the hour, the end of the day, or the end of the week, depending on the intensity of the crisis. Then focus everyone's energy and attention on driving execution to this designated point in time.

Anything that's not this clear, pinpointed outcome is noise. Starve the distractions. And do so with a fierceness that becomes contagious to everyone involved. Once your defined point is within reach, set your next point to pursue. And then continue the cadence—one by one, point to point.

Thomas Kolditz studies crisis professionals who spend their days working in harm's way. His findings validate the logic and efficacy of the point-to-point strategy: "People used to being in dangerous places learn to focus on the environment—they're not thinking about themselves. They're not focused on their own emotions. When you are task-focused, you're activating a different part of your brain than the part where you experience fear and anger. That helps keep them calm."[352]

When implementing a point-to-point strategy, others may feel the need to predefine multiple points in the future instead of a single one. Resist the temptation. Only focus on bridging the gap between the last point and the next point.

By shortening the time horizon in this way, you make the future feel more accessible, and that can make it seem less confusing and alarming. As Kolditz confirms, "If you give people an alternative future to the one that's occupying their fears, and you give them a sense of purpose, it helps."[353]

John Hudson, the chief survival instructor to the British military, advocates for the same logic of keeping individuals keenly focused on a clear, achievable task in a crisis. He believes it provides them with a sense of control and progress when they need it most.[354] As your organization surpasses one point of progress after the next, a sense of continuity, composure, and forward momentum begins to flow and grow.

PREDICT

With your organization stabilized thanks to a well-executed point-to-point strategy, it's time to anticipate what lies ahead. When it comes to forecasting, remember the cardinal rule: Trying to predict the future as a single point in time—X will happen on Y future date—is a fool's errand. Forecasting is about analyzing the probability of multiple futures.

Your job as a strategist is to have a working theory of things to come, a sense of how things may or may not change. Peter Thiel claims two things are always true about change: 1) Things will be different in the future than they are now, and 2) These changes will be rooted in today's world.[355] Start by anticipating how your organization would capitalize on new or different possibilities likely to emerge with this crisis.

For perspective, think back to the early stages of the pandemic. It represents one of the most unthinkable, disruptive events of the modern era. And yet it took only a matter of weeks, not months, to effectively predict greater opportunities associated with e-commerce, e-learning, remote work, telemedicine, zoom towns, and supply-chain solutions, among others. Such prediction is built on deep analysis, reflective study, and robust debates.

The first two stages, point and predict, are now under your belt. In pointing the way forward, you elevate the organization's focus above the chaos of the moment. In predicting what lies ahead, you unearth the opportunities and obstacles associated with change. Taken together, your organization is steady and ready.

Now it's time to pounce, converting a crisis into a breakthrough opportunity.

POUNCE

Dunigan O'Keeffe studies how companies emerge from a crisis.[356] Following the financial crisis of 2008, roughly 40 percent of S&P 500 companies dropped out of the index. These companies failed to effectively re-tool their strategy to adapt to the new normal. They spent too much time playing defense rather than offense. In O'Keefe's words, "History is unambiguous in showing that winners and losers are forged in the crucible of turbulence."[357]

AutoZone offers a telling example of how to navigate an altered landscape.[358]

The recession that followed the 2008 financial crisis prompted many Americans to delay or forgo purchasing new cars. This reality suggested more Americans needed their existing cars to last longer and run reliably.

If cars had to last longer and run well, a savvy forecaster could predict an uptick in maintenance and repair expenses. They could also anticipate the reluctance of cost-conscious consumers, still reeling from the recession, to take their cars to pricey mechanics or dealerships for help. A savvy forecaster could see these patterns and predict a tangible rise in do-it-yourself vehicle maintenance and repair.

Who better to convert this major crisis into a break-through opportunity than auto-part retailers who sell directly to customers? While other auto-part retailers may have connected these same dots, only AutoZone was ready to pounce with a winning strategy.[359]

By investing in better employee training and in-store technology, AutoZone deftly grew its suburban customer base. By increasing their private-label brand inventory to 50 percent of their offerings, AutoZone delivered lower prices on more items. And by expanding their video resources, AutoZone made it easier for customers to believe they could handle more of the maintenance and repair on their own. The result? AutoZone grew at a 50 percent higher rate than its best competitor, in addition to beating shareholder returns by ten points in the aftermath.

OURS VS. ITS

Before, during, or after a crisis, most organizations never think to ask: "Whose strategy do we want to manage during a crisis—ours or its?"

Think of a crisis as having a strategy all its own. It wants to operate on its terms. Go where it wants to go. Do what it wants to do. Say what it wants to say. A crisis doesn't want to be tamed by anyone or anything. It wants to pitch and make everyone else catch.

In bunker mode, organizations manage the crisis's strategy, not their own. They remain in a state of reaction. In coastguard mode, organizations manage their strategy to navigate the crisis. They remain in a state of anticipation, adaptation, and action.

If your organization wants to convert a crisis into a breakthrough opportunity, it needs a clear strategy to do so. But that's unlikely to happen unless you have a corps of capable strategists leading the way.

Strategists shine in a crisis. As things get worse, they get better. They don't panic. They don't rush. They don't argue with reality.[360] And they don't get overtaken by events.[361] Strategists stay disciplined, deliberate, and direct.

Importantly, strategists are never absent a strategy. They refuse to allow your organization to hunker down and hope for the best. They fight to carve the smartest path through the storm.

CONCLUSION

Scholars believe the history of literature can be pared down to only two plots: a stranger comes to town, or a hero goes on a journey.

This book speaks to both.

The strategist is a stranger to most individuals and organizations. They don't hear about strategists. They don't read about strategists. They don't think about strategists. They don't talk about strategists. And they don't solve for strategists. Be assured the strategy trap wants it no other way.

Yet treating the strategist as a stranger is clearly a losing strategy.

Left to its own devices, strategy struggles to be effective. For instance, one study shows 95 percent of employees don't understand their company's strategy.[362]

Before blaming employees, consider what's happening with senior leadership. Roughly 60 percent of organizations fail to link budget decisions to strategic priorities.[363] And no less than 85 percent of executives spend less than one hour per *month* on strategy.[364]

What's missing from this picture?

Yes, you guessed it: an army of strategists thriving at every level of these organizations. Strategists who believe strategy must be owned, not rented.

The bottom line: Strategies rise or fall based on strategists.

Having more and better strategists is the best way to deliver more and better strategies—just as having fewer strategists leads to less ownership and more failed strategies.

You have the opportunity, if not the responsibility, to convert the strategist's story from stranger to hero. There's no reason to wait.

HERO'S JOURNEY

The hero's journey is your story to show and tell.

If you're an accomplished strategist, this book gives voice and visibility to your fight against the status quo. If you're an aspiring strategist, this book delivers the beliefs and practices needed to live this identity into action.

Either way, the best way to be/become a strategist is to behave like a strategist.

Your performance becomes your practice. Your practice, daily and disciplined, builds your habits. Your habits feed your skills. Your skills inform your choices. Your choices illuminate your fixes. Your fixes clarify your mission. Your mission reinforces your identity. And your identity drives your destiny.

All of that flows with zero doubt about who you are, what you do, and why you matter.

Make no mistake: Being a strategist is hard work. Harder still is remaining a strategist in a world awash in reactive behavior. To cement the strategic and to guard against the nonstrategic, be militant with your focus. Concentrate on your code of behavior and its cadence: five habits, four skills, three choices, two fixes, one mission, and zero doubt.

Five Habits
Lead Time
Impose Clarity
Think in Questions
Push Upstream
See around Corners

Four Skills
Decide Better
Message Better
Innovate Better
Coach Better

Three Choices
Where to Play
When to Strike
How to Win

Two Fixes
Make Smart Bets
Secularize Strategy

One Mission
Solve for Strategists

Zero Doubt
Strategists First

Being a strategist is a deliberate choice—one you make every day, with every discussion and every decision. This intentionality requires discipline and focus. How do you maintain a forcefield of deep focus all around you?

Start by controlling what you can control.

No games. No drama. No ego. No excuses. And no default behaviors. Strategists know the best way to feed the essential is to starve the nonessential. As the strategist James Clear reaffirms, "Every action you take is a vote for the type of person you wish to become."[365]

Remember, the final stage of a hero's journey is to return home and share the wisdom of their travels. For strategists, this last stage represents a clarion call to coach.

You can't be a great strategist without also being a great coach.

Coach your team. Coach yourself. Get coached by an insider. Get coached by an outsider. Create a culture of coaching that feeds your entire organization.

THINKING: DEFAULT VS. DELIBERATE

In 2005, the writer David Foster Wallace delivered a memorable commencement speech at Kenyon College. He starts with a parable that only gets wiser with the passage of time:

> "There are these two young fish swimming along, and they happen to meet an older fish swimming the other way, who nods at them and says, 'Morning, boys, how's the water?' And the two young fish swim on for a bit, and then eventually one of them looks over at the other and goes, 'What the hell is water?'"[366]

For Wallace, the story symbolizes how the most obvious and essential realities are lost on some people. Here the older fish represents the power of awareness; the younger fish illustrate the curse of inattentiveness.

The younger fish fail on two fronts. First, they don't see the obvious: Water is everywhere. They are blind to context. Second, they don't understand the essential: More than their surroundings, water is their source of survival. They are ignorant of the truth.

Wallace ends his speech by asking graduates to keep obvious and essential realities top of mind. Don't be blind to context. Don't be ignorant of the truth. Above all, don't succumb to the distractions of life and fail to remind yourself that "this is water."[367]

Wallace's story captures the difference between deliberate thinking and default thinking.

Deliberate thinking means being aware of the obvious and the essential. Default thinking means going with the flow, unaware of the things that matter most. It's the surest way to spot a strategist from a non-strategist.

Strategists are deliberate thinkers and doers. Based on the obvious and the essential, they seek to maximize the present and anticipate the future. In doing so, they never stop reminding themselves to think and act like a strategist—their version of "this is water."

Non-strategists are default thinkers and doers. They simply react to whatever the status quo gives them. For them, the question "What the hell is water?" is a common occurrence.

Most organizations never ask if their strategies are born and raised on deliberate thinking or default thinking. Yet they can't escape the diverging results.

Default thinking leads to default strategies—ones that are bland, fragile, overhyped, and underwhelming. Deliberate thinking drives deliberate strategies—ones that are unique, choiceful, farsighted, agile, and effective.

Strategy professor Richard Rumelt describes the deliberateness of strategy this way: "Strategy means asking, or making, people do things that break with routine and focus collective effort and resources on new, or nonroutine, purposes."[368]

Or, in Wallace's words, being strategic means conditioning those around you to say, "This is water."[369]

If you want breakthrough success, create deliberate strategies.

If you want deliberate strategies, insist on deliberate thinking.

If you want deliberate thinking, nurture more and better strategists.

If you want more and better strategists, you must defeat the strategy trap at every turn.

FINAL VOCABULARY

The philosopher Richard Rorty believes every person has a final vocabulary.[370]

These are the words used to describe your current world. What makes them final is that you can't get beyond their performance to describe a new world—or new ways of thinking, doing, or being. Your current thinking can travel only as far as your current vocabulary allows.

To break free from current thinking and unlock new ways of thinking, you must develop a new vocabulary. Old words can't sufficiently convey the originality and totality of new ideas. It's why thousands of new words are created, recorded, and adopted every year. New concepts need new words to give them life, legitimacy, and longevity.

The other challenge to overcome with a final vocabulary is its staying power. If the only way to critique a final vocabulary is to do so within the confines of that same vocabulary, your ability to transcend it remains severely limited.

Rorty's theory of language reveals the uphill battle behind this book.

Most individuals and organizations have never known a vocabulary beyond strategy. Their current thinking about strategy is limited by their current language about strategy. It's why the strategist has never been more than a footnote in strategy's life and lexicon.

Strategy is ill-equipped to "free thought from what it silently thinks, and so enable it to think differently."[371]

Worse still, what happens when someone wants to question or critique strategy? They must do so on strategy's turf and with strategy's terms. That's the textbook definition of a home-field advantage. No wonder the strategy trap is so difficult to defeat.

More than ever, the world needs a new vocabulary for strategists.

New words spark new ideas. New ideas shape new beliefs. New beliefs ignite new actions. New actions drive new habits. New habits unleash new changes. And new changes unlock new frontiers of possibility.

All of that is needed to dethrone strategy and prioritize strategists. It's the only way strategists have a real chance to thrive and multiply.

Prior to the pandemic, organizations spent $35 billion a year on strategy consultants.[372] But what do they have to show for it, other than a mountain of subpar strategies and a chronic shortage of strategists?

Now imagine if these same organizations pushed upstream and invested $35 billion a year on activating, training, and supporting strategists. Talk about a game-changer.

Their numbers would be supersized. Their culture would be supercharged. Their strategies would be owned. And their impact would be lasting.

This book is a down payment on building a new vocabulary for strategists.

It's a directional effort designed to point, not prescribe. It's more compass, less map.

The aim is to unleash a legion of believers who see strategists for who they are: the world's most valuable, untapped resource.

So, yes, more and better words are needed for strategists.

But more of everything else too. More time. More clarity. More coaching. More resources. More support. More bets. More believers. More influence. More impact.

The one thing strategists don't need? More books idolizing strategy.

BONE-DEEP BELIEF

Few sayings rival the celebrity of this one: You must see it to believe it.

But what if the opposite were true? You must believe it to see it.

That's the premise of this book. Once you believe bone-deep in the strategist, you see strategy for what it is, not what it claims to be.

In reality, strategy fails far more often than it succeeds. Strategy is tired. Strategy is vain. Strategy is adrift. Above all, strategy is overmatched for the complexities that lie ahead.

The eighteenth-century political strategist Thomas Paine writes, "a long habit of not thinking a thing wrong, gives it a superficial appearance of being right."[373]

For fifty years, the world has not been thinking of the strategy trap as wrong. This default setting has given the strategy trap the superficial appearance of being right.

But strategy's wicked habit of sabotaging the strategist is bankrupt. And the time to save strategy from itself is long overdue.

Strategy must stop breathing its own exhaust and adopt a new reason for being. And that's to serve strategists, always and in all ways.

Strategists first.

That's the mission.

That's the mantra.

That's the magic.

If you remember one thing from this book, let it be this: **Putting strategists first is the only way strategy unlocks its full potential.**

BET ON YOU

This book is a bet on strategists. It's a bet on you.

The lifestyle strategist Tim Ferriss confirms, "Don't overestimate the world and underestimate yourself. You are better than you think."[374] Indeed.

You. Got. This.

Your identity is sure.

Your direction is set.

Your mission is clear.

Your tools are ready.

Your impact is needed.

Your time is now.

Always be you. Always be strategizing.

Strategists first.

EPILOGUE

Was this book useful to you? That was my job.

To get you where you need to go—faster, smarter, better. Learning if this book met your needs would be helpful.

Which parts of the book worked well for you?

Which parts failed you?

What's missing from a content perspective for you?

How can the writing be improved for you?

Such questions come from a short survey at www.ryanhays.com.

Beyond your feedback, I need your coaching. How can I become a better strategist in writing about strategists? Be assured, your coaching makes both of us better strategists.

More compass than map, this book points the way to a world where strategists are needed, welcomed, valued, and supported. What if you agree with the why behind this book but disagree with the how? What if you believe being a strategist requires a different set of habits, skills, and beliefs than those curated here?

Perfect. Now own it.

Build a framework that works for you. Convert your ideas into clear actions. Forge these actions into a discipline. And use this discipline to feed your focus on being a strategist—every day, every discussion, every decision.

Don't rent what I say. Own what you believe.

Strategists first.

The rest is, without fail, open to revision.

STRATEGIST'S NOTEBOOK

MODELS & METHODS

MODEL/ METHOD	FOCUS	DESCRIPTION
PEST	environmental scanning	PEST = Political, Economic, Sociocultural, Technological. A framework for analyzing the environmental factors that form the context for planning. Other variables, such as legal and ecological, may be included. Original version created by Francis Aguilar.
ADAPT	environmental scanning	ADAPT = Asymmetry, Disruption, Age, Polarization, Trust. A set of interdependent, accelerating forces shaping society. Created by PricewaterhouseCoopers.
SWOT	organizational analysis	SWOT = Strengths, Weaknesses, Opportunities, Threats. A framework for analyzing internal and external forces impacting an organization's viability and positioning. Created by Albert Humphrey.

7S Framework	**organizational planning**	7S = Strategy, Systems, Structure, Skills, Style, Staff, Shared Values. A model for assessing an organization's overall design, alignment, and viability. Created by Robert Waterman, Tom Peters, Tony Athos, and Richard Pascale.
BMI	**organizational planning**	BMI = Bureaucracy Mass Index. A model for assessing the degree of bureaucracy along seven organizational lines: bloat, friction, insularity, disempowerment, risk aversion, inertia, and politics. Created by Gary Hamel and Michele Zanini.
Kanri X Matrix	**organizational planning**	Integrated matrix designed to capture four foci on one page: long-term goals, annual objectives, top-level priorities, and metrics for improvement. Created by Hoshin Kanri.
BCG Matrix	**organizational planning**	A matrix for analyzing the strategic positioning and potential of business units per relative market share and speed of market growth. The four-quadrant iconography includes: stars, question marks, cash cows, and dogs. Created by Boston Consulting Group.

OGSM	**organizational planning**	OGSM = Objectives, Goals, Strategies, Metrics. A framework for planning and executing at various levels of an organization. Popularized by Procter & Gamble.
Scenario Planning	**organizational planning**	A model for anticipating potential futures and planning accordingly. Scenario planning includes both internal and external factors for analysis. Popularized by the Shell Corporation.
V2MOM	**organizational planning**	V2MOM = Vision, Values, Methods, Obstacles, Measures. A framework for guiding organizational leadership, alignment, and decision-making. Created by Mark Benioff and popularized by Salesforce.
Ansoff Matrix	**growth planning**	A framework for determining the optimal pathways for growth in existing and emerging markets. The four variables to the matrix include: market penetration, market development, product development, and diversification. Created by Igor Ansoff.
OKRs	**goal-setting**	OKRs = Objectives and Key Results. A framework for defining and tracking core aims and measured outcomes. Similar to Peter Drucker's concept of Management by Objectives (MBO). Created by Andy Grove.

SMART	goal-setting	SMART = Smart, Measurable, Attainable, Relevant, Time-Bound. A set of criteria used to create clarity in setting goals. Created by George Doran.
FAST	goal-setting	FAST = Frequently Discussed, Ambitious, Specific, Transparent. A set of criteria used to create clarity in setting goals. Created by Donald Sull and Charles Sull.
5 Whys	problem-solving	Iterative questioning technique designed to identify the root cause or defect of a problem by asking "why" five times in succession. Created by Sakichi Toyoda.
OODA Loop	decision-making	OODA = Observe, Orient, Decide, Act. A predefined cycle designed to enhance the speed and agility of decision-making. Created by John Boyd.
WRAP	decision-making	WRAP = Widen your options, Reality-test your assumptions, Attain distance before deciding, Prepare to be wrong. A process for guarding against biases in decision-making. Created by Chip Heath and Dan Heath.
DECIDE	decision-making	DECIDE = Define the problem, Establish the criteria, Consider all alternatives, Identify the best alternative, Develop a plan of action, Evaluate the solution. A framework for decision-making. Created by Kristina Guo.

RAPID	decision-making	RAPID = Recommender, Agreer, Performer, Inputter, Decider. A framework for assigning roles in the decision-making process. Created by Bain & Company.
5 Forces	competitive analysis	5 Forces = Power of buyers, Power of suppliers, Threat of substitutes, Threat of new entrants, Intensity of rivals. A method for analyzing the competitive landscape of an industry. Created by Michael Porter.
VRIO	competitive analysis	VRIO = Value, Rarity, Imitability, Organization. A framework for evaluating the competitive potential of resources and capabilities. Created by James Barney.
KPI	performance management	KPI = Key Performance Indicator. A method for evaluating the critical qualitative and quantitative performance metrics of a particular input or output. Created by Peter Drucker.
OKR	performance management	OKR = Objectives and Key Results. A method for defining goals and tracking outcomes. Created by Andy Grove.

Balanced Scorecard	performance management	A framework for defining, tracking, and assessing performance along four perspectives: financial, customer, internal business processes, and learning and growth. Created by Robert Kaplan and David Norton.
Gap Analysis	performance management	A framework for analyzing the gap between expected performance and actual results. Gap analysis includes three stages: identify the gaps between expected and actual, study the root causes behind the gaps, and create an improvement plan to bridge the gulf. Created by J. Michael Scott.
RACI	project management	RACI = Responsible, Accountable, Consulted, Informed. A matrix for clarifying roles and responsibilities in project management.
PDCA	continuous improvement	PDCA = Plan, Do, Check, Act. A method for continuous quality improvement. Created by W. Edwards Deming.
DMAIC	continuous improvement	DMAIC = Define, Measure, Analyze, Improve, Control. A method for continuous quality improvement typically associated with the Six Sigma model created by Bill Smith.

DIKAR	data management	DIKAR = Data, Information, Knowledge, Action, Results. A model for aligning technology and information management with organizational aims and ways. Created by N. Venkataraman.
MECE	data organization	MECE = Mutually Exclusive + Collectively Exhaustive. A logic for grouping information into subsets within a decision tree. Created by Barbara Minto.
Four Laws	change management	Four Laws of Behavior Change: Make it obvious, make it attractive, make it easy, and make it satisfying. A formula for nurturing good habits. Created by James Clear.
ADKAR	change management	ADKAR = Awareness, Desire, Knowledge, Ability, Reinforcement. A model for persuading individuals to change. Created by Jeff Hiatt.
Lewin's 3-Stage Model	change management	3-Stage Model = Unfreeze, Change, Refreeze. Focuses on the field that envelops change. Created by Kurt Lewin.
Kotter's 8-Step Process	change management	8-Step Process = Create urgency, Build a coalition, Form a strategic vision, Enlist a volunteer army, Enable action by removing barriers, Generate short-term wins, Sustain acceleration, Institute Change. A multistep process for managing change across complex organizations. Created by John Kotter.

Schneider Model	**change management**	Organizations function within four cultural archetypes: control culture, competence culture, collaboration culture, and cultivation culture. Any change-management effort must account for current culture, not just the desired culture. Created by William Schneider.
Eisenhower Matrix	**prioritizing**	Used to distinguish what is important versus what is urgent. If important and urgent, do it now. If important but not urgent, do it later. If not important but urgent, delegate it. If neither important nor urgent, don't do it. Inspired by Dwight Eisenhower.
SCAMPER	**innovating**	SCAMPER = Substitute, Combine, Adapt, Modify, Put to other use, Eliminate, Reverse. A framework for generating new ideas for products and services. Created by Bob Eberle.
SIT	**innovating**	SIT = Systematic Inventive Thinking. A framework for teaching creativity and innovation. The five techniques include: subtraction, division, multiplication, task unification, and attribute dependency. Created by Drew Boyd and Jacob Goldenberg.

DOI	**innovating**	DOI = Diffusion of Innovation Theory. A five-phase taxonomy for understanding how innovation spreads via adoption stages: Innovators, Early Adopters, Early Majority, Late Majority, and Laggards. Created by E. M. Rogers.
Google8	**innovating**	Google has eight pillars for innovation. 1) Have a mission that matters; 2) Think big but start small; 3) Strive for continual innovation, not instant perfection; 4) Look for ideas everywhere; 5) Share everything; 6) Spark with imagination; fuel with data; 7) Be a platform; and 8) Never fail to fail. First conceived by Susan Wojcicki.
SUCCESS	**messaging**	SUCCESS = Simple, Unexpected, Concrete, Credible, Emotional, Story. A formula for creating savvy messages that stick and persuade. Created by Chip Heath and Dan Heath.
STEPPS	**messaging**	STEPPS = Social currency, Triggered, Emotional, Public, Practically valuable, Stories. A formula for creating viral messages. Created by Jonah Berger.

OVERTON WINDOW	messaging	The range of ideas the mainstream public deems acceptable. This point of view scale goes from unthinkable to policy. Often referenced in political discourse and policy debates. Created by Joseph Overton.
STRONG	pitching	STRONG = Set the frame, Tell the story, Reveal the intrigue, Offer the prize, Nail the hookpoint, Get the deal. A formula for pitching ideas to decision makers. Created by Oren Klaff.
TEDW	questioning	TEDW = Tell me more, Explain why/how, Describe why/how, Walk me through. A technique for asking open-ended questions to facilitate more robust discussions. Created by Nikki Anderson.
QUESTION BURST	questioning	A technique for brainstorming in questions rather than in answers. Created by Hal Gregersen.
AAR	debriefing	AAR = After-Action Review. A structured process for studying a situation after the fact. Three areas of focus: What happened? Why did it happen? How can the effort by improved? Created by the US military.

4DX	executing	4DX = The Four Disciplines of Execution. 1) Focus on the Wildly Important; 2) Act on the Lead Measures; 3) Keep a Compelling Scorecard; 4) Create a Cadence of Accountability. A framework for optimizing your execution efforts. Created by Chris McChesney, Sean Covey, and Jim Huling.
4As	executing	4As = Alignment, Ability, Architecture, Agility. A framework for optimizing your execution efforts. Created by Scott Snell and Kenneth Carrig.
Hegelian Dialectic	thinking	A logic for reconciling opposing views. A dialectic includes three stages: thesis (stated idea), antithesis (negation of stated idea), synthesis (resolving difference between thesis and antithesis). Created by Georg Hegel. Popularized in strategy circles by Bob de Wit and Ron Meyer.
6 Thinking Hats	thinking	6 Thinking Hats = Facts (white), Feelings (red), Process (blue), Creativity (green), Benefits (yellow), Judgment (black). A framework for identifying different types of thinking. Created by Edward de Bono.

3Ps	coaching	3Ps = Project, Person, or Pattern of Behavior. A rubric for organizing and structuring questions for a coaching conversation. Created by Michael Bungay Stanier.
Drama Triangle	coaching	Drama Triangle = Victim, Rescuer, or Persecutor. A model for defining and analyzing subjectivity within drama-filled relationships. Created by Stephen Karpman.
HEART Framework	user experience	HEART = Happiness, Engagement, Adoption, Retention, Task Success. A framework for measuring the satisfaction of the user experience. Created by Google.
S = E x mc2	strategy formation	Strategy (S) equals execution (E) multiplied by market potential (m) and customer value (c) squared. A formula for developing and implementing strategy. Created by Brad Chase.
5Ps	strategy formation	5Ps = Strategy as plan, pattern, position, perspective, ploy. A taxonomy used to explain the multidimensionality of strategy work. Created by Henry Mintzberg.

Three Horizons	**strategy formation**	Three Horizons = Defend and extend core business (now), Nurture emerging business (near term), Create new business (future). A model for conceptualizing, structuring, and aligning levels of growth across time frames. Created by McKinsey.
Blue Ocean	**strategy formation**	A method for identifying and leveraging uncontested market space by creating a new value curve. Four questions for action: Which factors should be RAISED above industry standards? Which factors should be REDUCED below the standards? Which factors should be ELIMINATED? Which factors should be newly CREATED? Created by W. Chan Kim and Renee Mauborgne.
3Ds	**strategy formation**	3Ds = Diagnose, Decide, Deliver. A framework for developing and implementing strategy. Created by Greg Fisher, John Wisneski, and Rene Bakker.

4Cs	**strategy formation**	4Cs = Contrast, Combination, Constraint, Context. A framework for developing strategy. Contrast: What parts of the status quo are ripe for contradiction? Combination: What products or services can be combined in new or different ways? Constraint: What limitations can be converted to strengths? Context: How did a problem similar to yours get solved in a different context? Created by Adam Brandenburger.
ACCEPT	**strategy formation**	ACCEPT = Alignment, Clarity, Collaboration, Ease, Productivity, Time. A formula for simplifying strategy work. Created by Julia Hobsbawm.

NOTES

1   Franz Kafka, *Letters to Friends, Family, and Editors*.
     Translated by Richard Winston and Clara Winston (Berlin:
     Schocken Books, 1977), 16.

2   The lack of books and articles on the strategist is
     astonishing—especially given the popularity of strategy.
     Richard Rumelt's book *The Crux: How Leaders Become
     Strategists* (New York: Public Affairs, 2022) is the
     exception to the rule. Before that, a decade had passed
     since Cynthia Montgomery's book *The Strategist: Be the
     Leader Your Business Needs* (New York: HarperCollins,
     2012). But Montgomery's work speaks to current CEOs
     and aspiring CEOs, not to strategists at all levels of an
     organization. In 1982, Kenichi Ohmae authored *The
     Mind of the Strategist: The Art of Japanese Business* (New
     York: McGraw Hill, 1991). Recently, Roger Martin has
     been saying more about strategists in a series of strategy
     articles on *Medium*. Max McKeown at least references the
     strategist in his writings on strategy.

3   Ibid.

4   Robert Kaplan and David Norton, *The Strategy-Focused
     Organization: How Balanced Scorecard Companies Thrive
     in the New Business Environment* (Boston: Harvard
     Business School Press, 2001).

5   Calvin Tomkins, *Marcel Duchamp: The Afternoon
     Interviews* (New York: Badlands Unlimited, 2013), 93.

6   Cy Wakeman, *Reality-Based Leadership: Ditch the Drama,
     Restore Sanity to the Workplace, & Turn Excuses Into
     Results* (San Francisco: Jossey-Bass, 2010), 9–33.

7   Colin Powell, *It Worked for Me: In Life and Leadership*
     (United States: Harper, 2012), 146.

8   http://iranscope.ghandchi.com/Anthology/Alvin_
     Toffler00.htm

9   Jocko Willink and Leif Babin, *Extreme Ownership: How U.S. Navy SEALs Lead and Win* (New York: St. Martin's Press, 2017).

10 Guillermo Armando Ronda-Pupo and Luis Angel Guerras-Martin, "Dynamics of the evolution of the strategy concept 1962-2008: A co-word analysis," *Strategic Management Journal*, 33: 162–188 (2012).

11 Joan Magretta, *Understanding Michael Porter: the essential guide to strategy and competition* (Boston: Harvard Business Review Press, 2012), 20.

12 Richard Rumelt, *The Crux: How Leaders Become Strategists* (New York: Public Affairs, 2022), 5.

13 Max McKeown, *The Strategy Book*, 3rd Edition (United Kingdom: Pearson, 2020), xxiii.

14 Brad Chase, *Strategy First: How Businesses Win Big* (Austin: Greenleaf Book Group Press, 2020), 26.

15 Martin Reeves, Knut Haanes and Janmejaya Sinha, *Your Strategy Needs A Strategy: How to Choose and Execute the Right Approach* (Boston: Harvard Business Review Press, 2015), 6.

16 Roger Martin, "The Big Lie of Strategic Planning," *Harvard Business Review*, (2014).

17 Tim Luehrman, "Strategy as a Portfolio of Real Options," *Harvard Business Review*, (1998).

18 Bruce Henderson, "The Origin of Strategy," *Harvard Business Review*, (1989).

19 Greg Fisher, John Wisneski, and Rene Bakker, *Strategy in 3D: Essential Tools to Diagnose, Decide and Deliver* (New York: Oxford University Press, 2020), 8.

20 Gary Hamel, "Strategy as Revolution," *Harvard Business Review*, (1996).

21 Henry Mintzberg, Bruce Ahlstrand, and Joseph Lampel, *Strategy Safari: A Guided Tour Through the Wilds of Strategic Management* (New York: Free Press, 1998).

22 Ibid., 2–21.

23 Harvard Business Review, *HBR's ten must reads on strategy* (Boston: Harvard Business Review Press, 2011).

24 Richard Whittington, Patrick Regner, Duncan Angwin, Gerry Johnson, and Kevan Scholes, *Exploring Strategy: Text and Cases, 12th Edition* (United Kingdom: Pearson Education Limited, 2019).

25 James Clear, *Atomic Habits: An Easy & Proven Way to Build Good Habits & Break Bad Ones* (New York: Avery, 2018), 29–41.

26 Ibid., 33.

27 Ibid., 34–35.

28 Simon Sinek, *The Infinite Game*, (United States: Portfolio/ Penguin, 2019).

29 Robert Levine, *The Power of Persuasion: How We're Bought and Sold* (Hoboken: Wiley, 2003), 209.

30 Paul Leinwand, Cesare Mainardi, and Art Kleiner, "Only 8% of Leaders Are Good at Both Strategy and Execution," *Harvard Business Review*, (2015).

31 Roger Martin, "CEOs Should Stop Thinking Execution Is Somebody Else's Job; It Is Theirs," *Harvard Business Review*, (2017).

32 Ibid.

33 Graham Kenny, "5 Simple Rules for Strategy Execution," *Harvard Business Review*, (2019).

34 Ibid.

35 Rosabeth Moss Kanter, "Smart Leaders Focus on Execution First and Strategy Second," *Harvard Business Review*, (2017).

36 Ibid.

37 Ibid.

38 Ibid.

39 Michael Mankins, "5 Ways to Close the Strategy-Execution Gap," *Harvard Business Review*, (2017).

40 Ibid.

41   Paul Leinwand and Cesare Mainardi, *Strategy That Works: How Winning Companies Close the Strategy-to-Execution Gap* (Boston: Harvard Business Review Press, 2016).

42   Ibid.

43   Simon Horan and Michael Connerty, "Good Strategy Execution Requires Balancing 4 Tensions," *Harvard Business Review,* (2017).

44   Ricardo Viana Vargas and Edivandro Conforto, "Ten questions to help you turn strategy into reality," *The Chief Strategy Officer Playbook* by Brightline Project Management Institute (Great Britain: Brightline Project Management Institute, 2018), 34–37.

45   Ibid.

46   Gary Neilson, Karla Martin, and Elizabeth Powers, "The Secrets to Successful Strategy Execution," *Harvard Business Review,* (2008).

47   Ibid.

48   Larry Bossidy and Ram Charan, *Execution: The Discipline of Getting Things Done* (New York: Crown Business, 2000).

49   Clear, *Atomic Habits*, 24–25.

50   Rich Horwath, "The Strategic Thinking Manifesto," https://www.strategyskills.com/pdf/The-Strategic-Thinking-Manifesto.pdf?gclid=CIaV2fG0v88CFcVlfgodSBUM8A.

51   Steven Rogelberg, Cliff Scott and John Kello, "The Science and Fiction of Meetings," *MIT Sloan Management Review*, January 1, 2007.

52   The Radicati Group, "Email Statistics Report, 2020-2024," February 2020, https://www.radicati.com/wp/wp-content/uploads/2020/01/Email_Statistics_Report,_2020-2024_Executive_Summary.pdf.

53   Matt Plummer, "How to Spend Way Less Time on Email Every Day," *Harvard Business Review* (2019).

54   CPP, Inc., "Workplace Conflict and How Businesses Can Harness It to Thrive," CPP Global Human Capital Report,

July 2008, https://img.en25.com/Web/CPP/Conflict_
report.pdf.

55 Cal Newport, *Deep Work: Rules for Focused Success
in a Distracted World* (New York: Grand Central
Publishing, 2016).

56 Chris McChesney, Sean Covey, and Jim Huling, *The 4
Disciplines of Execution* (New York: Free Press, 2012).

57 Ibid.

58 Tim Ferriss, "The Tim Ferriss Show Transcripts:
Jim Collins (#361)," The Tim Ferriss Show,
February 20, 2019, https://tim.blog/2019/02/20/
the-tim-ferriss-show-transcripts-jim-collins-361/

59 Bronwyn Fryer, "Manage Your Time Like Jim Collins,"
Harvard Business Review, (2009).

60 Raymond Kethledge and Michael Erwin, *Lead Yourself
First: Inspiring Leadership Through Solitude* (New York:
Bloomsbury USA, 2017), 140–141.

61 Greg McKeown, *Essentialism: The Disciplined Pursuit of
Less* (United States: Crown, 2014).

62 Ibid., 22.

63 Ibid., 101.

64 Neil Pasricha, "Why You Need an Untouchable Day Every
Week," *Harvard Business Review*, (2018).

65 Kethledge and Erwin, *Lead Yourself First*, xvi.

66 Ibid.

67 John Donahoe, "To Beat the Chaos, Take a Thinking
Day," July 15, 2013 https://www.linkedin.com/
pulse/20130715110232-187399433-to-beat-the-chaos-
take-a-thinking-day/.

68 Michael Simmons, "5-Hour Rule: If you're not spending
5 hours per week learning, you're being irresponsible,"
Medium, October 12, 2017, https://medium.com/
accelerated-intelligence/the-5-hour-rule-if-youre-not-
spending-5-hours-per-week-learning-you-re-being-
irresponsible-791c3f18f5e6#:~:text=Top%20highlight-
,5%2DHour%20Rule%3A%20If%20you're%20not%20

spending%205,learning%2C%20you're%20being%20
irresponsible&text=%E2%80%9CIn%20my%20
whole%20life%2C%20I,Zero.%E2%80%9D&text=The-
%20answer%20is%20simple%3A%20Learning,time%20
that%20we%20can%20make.

69 Derek Thompson, "Inside X, Google's Moonshot Factory,"
    The Atlantic, November 15, 2017.

70 X – The Moonshot Factory, https://x.company.

71 Thompson, "Inside X."

72 Peter Diamandis and Steven Kotler, *Bold: How to Go Big,
    Achieve Success, and Impact the World* (New York: Simon
    & Schuster, 2015), 82.

73 Tim Hurson, *Think Better: An Innovator's Guide to
    Productive Thinking* (United Kingdom: McGraw-Hill
    Education, 2017), 45.

74 Daniel Kahneman, *Thinking, Fast and Slow* (United
    States: Farrar, Straus and Giroux, 2011). See also Daniel
    Kahneman, Oliver Sibony, and Cass Sunstein, *Noise: A
    Flaw in Human Judgement* (New York: Little, Brown and
    Company, 2021).

75 CNBC Money, "Charlie Munger: The Power of not making
    stupid decisions," August 4, 2017, https://www.cnbc.
    com/2017/08/04/charlie-munger-the-power-of-not-making-
    stupid-decisions.html.

76 Patrick Lencioni, *The Advantage: Why Organizational
    Health Trumps Everything Else In Business* (United
    Kingdom: Wiley, 2012), 73–172.

77 Ibid., 77.

78 Roger Martin, "Strategic Choice Chartering," Medium,
    November 9, 2020, https://medium.com/the-innovation/
    strategic-choice-chartering-3d56d8962ec3.

79 Lencioni, *The Advantage,* 15.

80 John Rossman, *Think like Amazon: 50 ½ ideas to
    become a digital leader* (New York: McGraw-Hill,
    2019), 235--237.

81 Ibid.

82 Ibid., 235.
83 Ibid.
84 Ibid., 238.
85 Ibid., 6.
86 Jim VandeHei, Mike Allen, and Roy Schwartz, *Smart Brevity: The Power of Saying More With Less* (New York: Workman Publishing, 2022).
87 Ibid., 12.
88 Debbie Millman, *Why Design Matters: Conversations with the World's Most Creative People* (New York: Harper Design, 2022), 187.
89 Michel Foucault, *The Use of Pleasure: Volume 2 of The History of Sexuality* (New York: Vintage Books, 1990), 9.
90 Powell, *It Worked for Me* ,116.
91 Warren Berger, *A More Beautiful Question: The Power of Inquiry to Spark Breakthrough Ideas* (United States: Bloomsbury USA, 2014).
92 Thompson, "Inside X."
93 Warren Berger, *The Book of Beautiful Questions: The Powerful Questions That Will Help You Decide, Create, Connect, and Lead* (United States: Bloomsbury Publishing, 2018).
94 Hal Gregersen, "Better Brainstorming," *Harvard Business Review*, (2018).
95 Hal Gregersen, *Questions Are the Answer: A Breakthrough Approach to Your Most Vexing Problems at Work and in Life* (United States: Harper Business, 2018).
96 John Hagel, "Good Leadership Is About Asking Good Questions," *Harvard Business Review*, (2021).
97 Eric Schmidt, Jonathan Rosenberg and Alan Eagle, *Trillion Dollar Coach: The Leadership Playbook of Silicon Valley's Bill Campbell* (New York: Harper Business, 2019), 90.
98 Gregersen, "Better Brainstorming."
99 Leigh Buchanan, "100 Great Questions Every Entrepreneur Should Ask," *Inc. Magazine*, (2014), https://www.inc.com/

magazine/201404/leigh-buchanan/100-questions-business-leaders-should-ask.html.

100 Montgomery, *The Strategist,* 56.

101 Jillian D'Onfro, "Jeff Bezos' brilliant advice for anyone running a business," *Business Insider,* January 31, 2015, https://www.businessinsider.com/jeff-bezos-brilliant-advice-for-anyone-running-a-business-2015-1.

102 Walter Frick, "The 'career-making' question that will help you make better decisions," *Quartz,* September 6, 2020, https://qz.com/work/1899543/asking-this-question-will-help-you-make-better-career-decisions/.

103 Ibid.

104 Ibid.

105 Joel Lovell, "Colum McCann's Radical Empathy," *New York Times,* May 30, 2013, https://www.nytimes.com/2013/06/02/magazine/colum-mccanns-radical-empathy.html#:~:text=No%20windows%2C%20two%20very%20tight,that%20we%20hesitated%20to%20speak.

106 Simon Sinek, *Start with Why: How Great Leaders Inspire Everyone to Take Action* (United Kingdom: Portfolio/Penguin, 2011).

107 Steven Johnson, *Farsighted: How We Make the Decisions That Matter the Most* (United States: Penguin Publishing Group, 2018).

108 Ibid.

109 Ibid., 120.

110 Ibid., 121.

111 Ibid.

112 Ibid., 122.

113 Reed Hastings and Erin Meyer, *No Rules Rules: Netflix and the Culture of Reinvention* (United States of America: Random House, 2020), 210–218.

114 Ibid., 212.

115 Barack Obama, "How I Approach the Toughest Decisions," Medium, December 9, 2020, https://barackobama.medium.com/how-i-approach-the-toughest-decisions-dc1b165cdf2d.

116 John Kenneth Galbraith, *A Contemporary Guide to Economics, Peace, and Laughter* (Boston: Houghton Mifflin Company, 1971), 50.

117 Powell, *It Worked for Me*, 91.

118 Ibid.

119 Rumelt, *The Crux*, 55.

120 Ibid., 40–41.

121 Ibid., 9.

122 Dan Heath, *Upstream: The Quest to Solve Problems Before They Happen* (United States: Avid Reader Press/ Simon & Schuster, 2020).

123 Ibid., 17.

124 Ibid., 2.

125 Ibid., 1–5.

126 Ibid.

127 Ibid., 3.

128 Ibid., 23.

129 Ibid., 39-55.

130 Rossman, *Think like Amazon*, 107.

131 Cormac McCarthy, *The Road* (New York: Vintage Books, 2006), 140.

132 Christiane Lemieux and Duff McDonald, *Frictionless: Why the Future of Everything Will Be Fast, Fluid, and Made Just for You* (United States: Harper Business, 2020).

133 Ibid., 1–8; 254

134 John Rossman, *Think Like Amazon: 50 1/2 Ideas to Become a Digital Leader* (Greece: McGraw-Hill Education, 2019), 128.

135 Ibid., 49.

136 Ibid., 49–53.

137 Ibid., 128; 187.

138 Ibid.

139 Ibid., 187.

140 Ibid.

141 Monica Chin, "Meet the 24-year-old who's tracking every broken McDonald's ice-cream machine in the US,"

The Verge, October 22, 2020, https://www.theverge.com/2020/10/22/21529477/mcdonalds-mcbroken-bot-ice-cream-machines-app-engineering.

142 Tom Huddleston, "The winner of Warren Buffett's March Madness office pool could get $1 million a year for life," *CNBC*, March 21, 2019, https://www.cnbc.com/2019/03/21/inside-warren-buffetts-multimillion-dollar-march-madness-challenge.html.

143 Philip Tetlock and Dan Gardner, *Superforecasting: The Art and Science of Prediction* (New York: Broadway Books, 2015), 4.

144 Philip Tetlock, *Expert Political Judgement: How Good Is It? How Can We Know?* (Princeton: Princeton University Press, 2005).

145 Tetlock and Gardner, *Superforecasting*, 1–23.

146 Ibid., 279.

147 Ibid., 127.

148 Ibid., 201.

149 Hastings and Meyer, *No Rules Rules*, xi–xiii. See also Minda Zetlin, "Blockbuster Could Have Bought Netflix for $50 Million, but the CEO Thought It Was a Joke," *Inc. Magazine*, September 20, 2019, https://www.inc.com/minda-zetlin/netflix-blockbuster-meeting-marc-randolph-reed-hastings-john-antioco.html.

150 Zetlin, "Blockbuster Could Have Bought Netflix for $50 Million."

151 Tetlock and Gardner, *Superforecasting,* 273.

152 Ram Charan, *The Attacker's Advantage: Turning Uncertainty into Breakthrough Opportunities* (New York: PublicAffairs, 2015).

153 Ibid., 31.

154 Michael Porter, "How Competitive Forces Shape Strategy," *Harvard Business Review*, (1979).

155 Michael Porter, *Competitive Strategy* (New York: Free Press, 1980).

156 Michael Porter, "What is Strategy?," *Harvard Business Review*, (1996).

157 Joan Magretta, *Understanding Michael Porter: The Essential Guide to Competition and Strategy* (Cambridge: Harvard Business Review Press, 2011).

158 Ibid., 20.

159 Ibid., 184.

160 Ibid., 52.

161 Cassie Kozyrkov, "The problem with analyzing policy decisions in hindsight," Medium, May 26, 2020, https://medium.com/swlh/the-problem-with-analyzing-policy-decisions-in-hindsight-5f5632c6bc0b.

162 Annie Duke, *Thinking in Bets: Making Smarter Decisions When You Don't Have All the Facts* (New York: Portfolio, 2018).

163 Ibid., 90.

164 Ibid.

165 Adam Grant, *Think Again: The Power of Knowing What You Don't Know* (New York: Viking, 2021), 218.

166 Duke, *Thinking in Bets*, 180.

167 Lars Lefgren, Brennan Platt, and Joseph Price, "Sticking with What (Barely) Worked: A Test of Outcome Bias," *Management Science* 61, no. 5 (2015): 1121–1136.

168 Ibid., 1122.

169 Jeff Bezos, 1997 Letter to Shareholders, https://s2.q4cdn.com/299287126/files/doc_financials/annual/2016-Letter-to-Shareholders.pdf.

170 Ibid.

171 Ibid.

172 Grant Hammond, *The Mind of War: John Boyd and American Security* (Washington: Smithsonian Press, 2001). See also Lawrence Freedman, *Strategy: A History* (New York: Oxford University Press, 2013), 196–199.

173 Hammond, *The Mind of War*, 322–323.

174 Bezos, 1997 Letter.

175 Ibid.

176 Ibid.

177 Ibid.

178 Steven Johnson, *Farsighted: How We Make the Decisions That Matter the Most* (New York: Riverhead Books, 2018), 56.

179 Adam Grant, *Think Again: The Power of Knowing What You Don't Know* (New York: Viking, 2021).

180 Ibid., 28.

181 Ibid.

182 Duke, *Thinking in Bets*, 94.

183 Ibid., 37–117.

184 Ibid., 28.

185 Natalie Goldberg, *Writing Down the Bones: Freeing the Writer Within* (Boulder: Shambhala Publications, 2016), 53.

186 George Lakoff, *Don't Think of an Elephant! Know Your Values and Frame the Debate* (United States: Scribe, 2005).

187 Kahneman, *Thinking, Fast and Slow*, 52.

188 Jonah Berger, Marc Meredith, and S. Christian Wheeler, "Contextual Priming: Where People Vote Affects How They Vote," *The Proceedings of the National Academy of Sciences (PNAS)* 105 (2008): 8846–49.

189 Solomon Asch, "Forming impressions of personality," *The Journal of Abnormal and Social Psychology* 41.3 (1946): 258.

190 Sara Solnick and David Hemenway, "Is more always better?: A survey on positional concerns," *Journal of Economic Behavior & Organization*, 37 (1998): 373–383.

191 *Frontline*, "Interview: Clotaire Rapaille," December 15, 2003, https://www.pbs.org/wgbh/pages/frontline/shows/persuaders/interviews/rapaille.html.

192 Howard Schultz, *From the Ground Up: A Journey To Reimagine The Promise of America* (New York: Random House, 2019), xi.

193 Ibid., 27.

194 Ibid., 31.

195 Kahneman, *Thinking, Fast and Slow*, 269–363.

196 Frank Luntz, *Words That Work: It's Not What You Say, It's What People Hear* (New York: Hyperion, 2007), 164–66.

197 Ibid., 165.

198 Howard Schultz, *Onward: How Starbucks Fought for Its Life without Losing Its Soul* (New York: Harmony/Rodale, 2012), 142.

199 Chip Heath and Karla Starr, *Making Numbers Count: The Art and Science of Communicating Numbers* (New York: Avid Reader Press, 2022).

200 Ibid., 52.

201 Ibid., 132.

202 Chip Heath and Dan Heath, *Made to Stick: Why Some Ideas Survive and Others Die* (New York: Random House, 2007).

203 Jonah Berger, *Contagious: Why Things Catch On* (New York: Simon & Schuster, 2013).

204 Robert Zajonc, "Mere Exposure: A Gateway to the Subliminal," *Current Directions in Psychological Science*, 10 (6): 224–228 (2001).

205 https://www.quora.com/What-is-Amazons-approach-to-product-development-and-product-management.

206 Ibid.

207 Rossman, *Think like Amazon*, 242.

208 Ibid.

209 David Yoffie and Michael Cusumano, *Strategy Rules: Five Timeless Lessons From Bill Gates, Andy Grove and Steve Jobs* (New York: Harper Business, 2015), 23.

210 Duleesha Kulasooriya, John Hagel, John Seely Brown, and Peter Williams, "Scaling Edges: A pragmatic pathway to broad internal change," *Deloitte Insights*, 2012, https://www2.deloitte.com/content/dam/Deloitte/au/Documents/technology/deloitte-au-tech-center-scaling-edges-paper-151014.pdf.

211 Ibid.

212 Ibid., 17–19; 24–36.

213 Debbie Millman, *Why Design Matters: Conversations with The World's Most Creative People* (New York: Harper Design, 2021), 331.

214 Ibid., 31.

215 Ibid., 26.

216 Walter Isaacson, *Steve Jobs* (New York: Simon & Schuster, 2011), 115.

217 Ibid., 144.

218 The Garage, Microsoft, https://www.microsoft.com/en-us/garage/

219 X – The Moonshot Factory.

220 Scott Anthony, "Kodak's Downfall Wasn't About Technology," *Harvard Business Review*, (2016).

221 Ibid.

222 Diamandis and Kotler, *Bold*, 3–22.

223 Ibid., 6.

224 Kurt Vonnegut, *Player Piano* (New York: Random House, 1952), 86.

225 Adam Bradenburger, "Strategy Needs Creativity," *Harvard Business Review*, (2019).

226 Ibid.

227 Rumelt, *The Crux*, 29.

228 Mike Krzyzewski, *The Gold Standard* (New York: Grand Central Publishing, 2009), 2.

229 Ibid.

230 Netflix Culture — Seeking Excellence, Netflix, https://jobs.netflix.com/culture.

231 Ibid.

232 Hastings and Meyer, *No Rules Rules*, 245–277.

233 Ibid., 52.

234 Ibid., 254.

235 Ibid.

236 Schmidt, Eagle, and Rosenberg, *Trillion Dollar Coach*, 188.

237 Michael Bungay Stanier, *The Coaching Habit: Say Less, Ask More & Change the Way You Lead Forever* (Toronto: Box of Crayons Press, 2016).

238 Michael Norton, Daniel Mochon, and Dan Ariely, "The IKEA Effect: When Labor Leads to Love," *Journal of Consumer Psychology* 22, no. 3: 453–460 (July 2012).

239 Ibid.

240 Martin Hirt, "Could Roger Federer be as successful playing badminton?," Strategy & Corporate Finance Blog, March 26, 2018, https://www.mckinsey.com/business-functions/strategy-and-corporate-finance/our-insights/the-strategy-and-corporate-finance-blog/could-roger-federer-be-as-successful-playing-badminton.

241 Ibid.

242 Reeves, Haanes, and Sinha, *Your Strategy Needs A Strategy*.

243 Simon Ramo, *Extraordinary Tennis for the Ordinary Player* (New York: Crown, 1973).

244 See Yoffie and Cusumano, 47.

245 Raja Rajamannar, *Quantum Marketing: Mastering the New Marketing Mindset for Tomorrow's Consumers* (New York: HarperCollins Leadership), 48.

246 Jeff Haden, "20 Years Ago, Jeff Bezos Said This 1 Thing Separates People Who Achieve Lasting Success From Those Who Don't," *Inc. Magazine*, November 6, 2017.

247 Ibid.

248 Ibid.

249 McKeown, *The Strategy Book*, 54.

250 Sam Walton, *Sam Walton: Made in America* (New York: Doubleday, 1992).

251 Jennifer Reingold, "P&G Chairman A.G. Lafley Steps Down—For Good, This Time?," *Fortune*, June 1, 2016.

252 A.G. Lafley and Roger Martin, *Playing to Win: How Strategy Really Works* (Boston: Harvard Business Review Press, 2013).

253 Ibid., 3.

254 Ibid., 5.

255 Ibid., 36.

256 Ibid., 93.

257 Ibid., 97.

258 Ibid., 112.

259 Ibid., 119.

260 Ibid., 114.

261 Ibid., 129.

262 Ibid., 136.

263 Ibid., 139.

264 Adam Grant, *Originals: How Non-Conformists Move the World* (New York: Penguin Books, 2016), 107.

265 Ibid.

266 Lisa Kahn, "The Long-Term Labor Market Consequences of Graduating from College in a Bad Economy," *Labour Economics* 17, no. 2 (2010): 303–16.

267 Bill Gross, TED Talk, March 2015.

268 Ibid.

269 Daniel Pink, *When: The Scientific Secrets of Perfect Timing* (New York: Riverhead Books, 2018).

270 Ibid., 94.

271 Ibid.

272 Ibid., 147.

273 Ibid.

274 Ibid., 145–152.

275 Ibid., 149.

276 Ibid., 145–164.

277 Ibid., 124–128.

278 Ibid., 127.

279 Rita McGrath, *Seeing Around Corners: How to Spot Inflection Points in Business Before They Happen* (Boston: Houghton Mifflin Harcourt, 2019).

280 Ibid., 6.

281 Ibid., 13–64.

282 See Gross.

283 Neal Cabage, "Why Timing Is Everything," *Inc. Magazine*, May 30, 2013.

284 Steven Johnson, *Where Good Ideas Come From: The Natural History of Innovation* (New York: Riverhead

Books, 2011). Johnson borrows this concept from the biologist Stuart Kauffman.

285 Rory McDonald and Robert Bremner, "When It's Time to Pivot, What's Your Story?," *Harvard Business Review*, (2020).

286 Ibid.

287 Langer, Blank, and Chanowitz, "The mindlessness of ostensibly thoughtful action: The role of "placebic" information in interpersonal interaction," Journal of Personality and Social Psychology, 36(6), (1978), 635–642.

288 Ibid.

289 Martin Hirt, "Why your business needs a hit mentality," Strategy & Corporate Finance Blog, October 24, 2018, https://www.mckinsey.com/business-functions/strategy-and-corporate-finance/our-insights/the-strategy-and-corporate-finance-blog/why-your-business-needs-a-hit-mentality.

290 James Allen, "The Changing Nature of Strategy: Reflections on Thirty Years," Founder's Mentality Blog, February 7, 2019, https://www.bain.com/insights/the-changing-nature-of-strategy-reflections-on-thirty-years-fm-blog/.

291 Hamel, "Strategy as Revolution."

292 John Cook, "Jeff Bezos on innovation: Amazon 'willing to be misunderstood for long periods of time,'" *GeekWire*, June 7, 2011, https://www.geekwire.com/2011/amazons-bezos-innovation/.

293 Orit Gadiesh and James Gilbert, "Transforming Corner-Office Strategy into Frontline Action," *Harvard Business Review*, (2001).

294 Ibid.

295 Lafley and Martin, *Playing to Win*, 156.

296 Flyvbjerg, Bent, 2021, "Top Ten Behavioral Biases in Project Management: An Overview," *Project Management Journal*, 52, 6, 531–546.

297 *The Portable Nietzsche,* translated by Walter Kaufmann (New York City: The Viking Press, 1968), 556.
298 Roger Martin, "The First Question to Ask of Any Strategy," *Harvard Business Review,* (2015).
299 Ibid.
300 See Cook.
301 Joe Fig, *Inside the Painter's Studio* (Princeton: Princeton Architectural Press, 2009), 42.
302 Ibid.
303 Jim Collins, *Turning the Flywheel: A Monograph to Accompany Good to Great* (United Kingdom: Harper Collins, 2019).
304 Ibid., 1.
305 Ibid., 9.
306 Ibid., 4.
307 Ibid., 18.
308 Ryoji Kimura, Martin Reeves, and Kevin Whitaker, "The New Logic of Competition," *Featured Insights,* March 22, 2019, https://www.bcg.com/en-us/publications/2019/new-logic-of-competition.
309 Todd Zenger, "The Disney Recipe," *Harvard Business Review,* (2013).
310 Roger Martin, "The Big Lie of Strategic Planning," *Harvard Business Review,* (2014).
311 Ibid.
312 Ibid.
313 Duke, *Thinking in Bets,* 3.
314 Ibid., 22.
315 Martin, "The Big Lie of Strategic Planning."
316 Sven Smit, "Why strategy is like poker, not golf," Strategy & Corporate Finance Blog February 8, 2018, https://www.mckinsey.com/business-functions/strategy-and-corporate-finance/our-insights/the-strategy-and-corporate-finance-blog/why-strategy-is-like-poker-not-like-golf.
317 Ibid.

318 Hirt.

319 Ibid.

320 Paul Sawers, "YouTube revenue shows its potential as a standalone company," *VentureBeat*, February 4, 2020.

321 Hastings and Meyer, *No Rules Rules*, 230.

322 Ibid.

323 Goldberg, *Writing Down the Bones*, 35.

324 John Hagel and John Seely Brown, "Take a Zoom Out, Zoom In Approach to Business Strategy," *The Wall Street Journal*, July 27, 2018, https://deloitte.wsj.com/riskandcompliance/2018/07/27/take-a-zoom-out-zoom-in-approach-to-business-strategy/.

325 Ibid.

326 Ibid.

327 John Hagel and John Seely Brown, "Zoom out/zoom in: An alternative approach to strategy in a world that defies prediction," *Deloitte Insights*, 2018, https://www2.deloitte.com/content/dam/insights/us/articles/4615_Zoom-out-zoom-in/DI_Zoom-out-zoom-in.pdf.

328 Donald Sull, Charles Sull, and James Yoder, "No One Knows Your Strategy—Not Even Your Top Leaders," *MIT Sloan Management Review*, (2018).

329 Ibid.

330 Ibid.

331 Ibid.

332 Fisher, Wisneski, and Bakker, *Strategy in 3D*, 15. See also Hamel, "Strategy as Revolution." See also Rita McGrath, *Seeing Around Corners: How to Spot Inflection Points in Business Before They Happen* (Boston: Houghton Mifflin Harcourt, 2019). See also A. G. Lafley and Roger Martin, *Playing To Win: How Strategy Really Works* (Boston: Harvard Business Review Press, 2013). See also Stephen Wall and Shannon Rye Wall, *The New Strategists: Creating Leaders at All Levels* (New York: The Free Press, 1995). See also *Humanocracy: Creating Organizations as Amazing as the People Inside Them* (Boston: Harvard Business

Review Press, 2020). See also Robert Kabacoff, "Develop Strategic Thinkers Throughout Your Organization," *Harvard Business Review*, (2014).

333 Christian Stadler, Julia Hautz, Kurt Matzler, and Stephan Friedrich Von Den Eichen, *Open Strategy: Mastering Disruption From Outside the C-Suite* (Cambridge: The MIT Press, 2021).

334 Lafley and Martin, *Playing To Win*, 50; 138.

335 Ibid., 138.

336 Ibid.

337 Schmidt, Eagle, and Rosenberg, *Trillian Dollar Coach*, 188.

338 Teppo Felin, "When Strategy Walks Out the Door," *MIT Sloan Management Review*, (2016).

339 See Montgomery, *The Strategist*. See also Rumelt, *The Crux*.

340 "Faulkner: Advice to a Young Writer," *The Daily Princetonian*, March 19, 1958, https://theprince.princeton.edu/princetonperiodicals/?a=d&d=Princetonian19580319-01.1.2&e=-------en-20--1--txt-txIN-march+19%2c+1958.

341 "Leadership Principles," Amazon, https://www.amazon.jobs/en/principles.

342 "Did Peter Drucker Say That?," Drucker Institute, https://www.drucker.institute/did-peter-drucker-say-that/

343 Roger Martin, "The Execution Trap," *Harvard Business Review*, (2010).

344 Roger Martin, "Stop Distinguishing Between Execution and Strategy," *Harvard Business Review*, (2015).

345 Danny Miller, *The Icarus Paradox: How Exceptional Companies Bring About Their Own Downfall* (New York: Harper Business, 1990).

346 Drew Boyd and Jacob Goldenberg, *Inside the Box: A Proven System of Creativity for Breakthrough Results* (United Kingdom: Simon & Schuster, 2014). For this notion of using constraints to foster creativity, see also Scott Sonenshein, *Stretch: Unlock the Power of Less—*

and Achieve More Than You Ever Imagined (New York: Harper Business, 2017).

347 Paul Polman and Andrew Winston, *Net Positive: How Courageous Companies Thrive By Giving More Than They Take* (Boston: Harvard Business Review Press, 2021), xi.

348 Paul Leinwand, Nils Naujok, and Joachim Rotering, "Memo to the CEO: Is you're your chief strategy officer set up for success?," Strategy+business, January 15, 2019," https://www.strategy-business.com/article/Memo-to-the-CEO-Is-Your-Chief-Strategy-Officer-Set-Up-for-Success.

349 Max De Pree, *Leadership is an art* (New York: Doubleday, 1989), 87.

350 Charan, *The Attacker's Advantage*, 3–4.

351 Ibid., 4.

352 Jena McGregor, "The extreme leadership that got the Thai soccer boys out of the cave alive," *The Washington Post*, July 10, 2018, https://www.washingtonpost.com/news/on-leadership/wp/2018/07/10/the-extreme-leadership-that-got-the-thai-soccer-boys-out-of-the-cave/.

353 Ibid.

354 John Hudson, *How to Survive: Lessons for Everyday Life from the Extreme World* (United Kingdom: Macmillan, 2019).

355 Peter Thiel, *Zero to One: Notes on startups, or How to Build the Future* (New York: Crown Business, 2014), 6.

356 Dunigan O'Keeffe, "Retooling Strategy for a Post-Pandemic World," *Bain Insights*, July 22, 2020, https://www.bain.com/insights/retooling-strategy-for-a-post-pandemic-world/.

357 Ibid.

358 Kermit King, Dan Wald, and Justin Manly, "Advantage Beyond the Crisis," April 21, 2020, https://www.bcg.com/en-us/publications/2020/building-business-advantage-beyond-covid-19-crisis.

359 Ibid.

360 Wakeman, *Reality-Based Leadership*, 9–33.

361 Powell, *It Worked for Me*, 146.
362 Robert Kaplan and David Norton, "The Office of Strategy Management," *Harvard Business Review* (2005).
363 Ibid.
364 Ibid.
365 Clear, *Atomic Habits*, 38.
366 David Foster Wallace, *This Is Water: Some Thoughts, Delivered on a Significant Occasion, about Living a Compassionate Life* (New York: Little, Brown and Company, 2009).
367 Ibid.
368 Rumelt, *The Crux*, 111.
369 Wallace, *This Is Water*.
370 Richard Rorty, *Contingency, irony, and solidarity* (United Kingdom: Cambridge University Press, 1989).
371 Foucault, *The Use of Pleasure*.
372 E. Mazareanu, "Size of Global Consulting Market from 2011 to 2020, by Segment," Statista, December 10, 2019.
373 Thomas Paine, *Common Sense* (Philadelphia: Robert Bell Publishing, 1776).
374 Tim Ferriss, *Tools of Titans: The Tactics, Routines, and Habits of Billionaires, Icons, and World-Class Performers* (Boston: Houghton Mifflin Harcourt, 2017), 201.

ABOUT THE AUTHOR

Photo by Andrew Higley

Ryan Hays has been doing strategy work for more than two decades at some of the nation's leading academic institutions, including Dartmouth, Emory and Princeton. During this time, he has provided strategic counsel to multiple university presidents and governing boards and coauthored several strategic plans. He currently serves as executive vice president and chief innovation and strategy officer at the University of Cincinnati.

Hays received a BA from DePauw University and a PhD in psychoanalytic studies and postmodern theory from Emory University. His dissertation on Sigmund Freud has ranked among the top 25 Most-Accessed Dissertations and Theses on ProQuest, an electronic library of more than 2 million dissertations and theses.